MARCO POLO

D1150383

CU BA

USA
Gulf of Mexico
BAHAMAS
ATLANTIC OCEAN
Havana
MEXICO
CUBA
DOM. REPUBLIC
HAITI
BELIZE
JAMAICA
HONDURAS
Caribbean Sea
NICARAGUA
VENEZUELA
COLOMBIA
PANAMÁ

www.marco-polo.com

FREE!

THE
TOURING APP

shows you the way ...
including routes and offline maps!

GET MORE OUT OF YOUR MARCO POLO GUIDE

IT'S AS SIMPLE AS THIS

1 go.marco-polo.com/cub

2 download and discover

GO!

WORKS OFFLINE!

6 **INSIDER TIPS**
Our top 15 Insider Tips

8 **BEST OF...**
   ● Great places for free
   ● Only on Cuba
   ● And if it rains?
   ● Relax and chill out

12 **INTRODUCTION**
Discover Cuba!

18 **WHAT'S HOT**
There are lots of new things to
discover on Cuba

20 **IN A NUTSHELL**
Background information on
Cuba

26 **FOOD & DRINK**
Top culinary tips

30 **SHOPPING**
For a fun-filled shopping spree!

32 **HAVANA**

50 **THE WEST**
51 Pinar del Río 54 Valle de
Viñales 56 Varadero

62 **THE CENTRE**
63 Camagüey 66 Cienfuegos
68 Jardines del Rey 70 Santa
Clara 72 Trinidad

74 **THE EAST**
75 Baracoa 77 Holguín
80 Santiago de Cuba

SYMBOLS

INSIDER TIP	Insider Tip
★	Highlight
●●●●	Best of...
᛬	Scenic view
♲	Responsible travel: for eco-logical or fair trade aspects
(*)	Telephone numbers that are not toll-free

**PRICE CATEGORIES
HOTELS**

Expensive	over 120 CUC
Moderate	60–120 CUC
Budget	under 60 CUC

Prices for one night in a
double room for two people
without breakfast

**PRICE CATEGORIES
RESTAURANTS**

Expensive	over 30 CUC
Moderate	18–30 CUC
Budget	under 18 CUC

Prices for a meal (starter,
main dish, dessert) without
drinks

88 **DISCOVERY TOURS**
88 Cuba at a glance 94 The green west: Orchids, cork oaks and lime mountains
97 To the cayos and playas on the northern coast 100 Where it all began: Round trip from Costa Esmeralda

114 **LINKS, BLOGS, APPS & MORE**
Plan ahead and use on the go

116 **TRAVEL TIPS**
From A to Z

122 **USEFUL PHRASES**

126 **ROAD ATLAS**

104 **SPORTS & ACTIVITIES**
Activities for all seasons

108 **TRAVEL WITH KIDS**
Best things to do with kids

112 **FESTIVALS & EVENTS**
All dates at a glance

138 **INDEX & CREDITS**

140 **DOS & DON'TS**

DID YOU KNOW?
Timeline → p. 14
For bookworms & film buffs → p. 24
Local specialities → p. 28
Gods, cults and saints → p. 83
National holidays → p. 112
Budgeting → p. 117
Currency converter → p. 119
Weather → p. 120

MAPS IN THE GUIDEBOOK
(128 A1) Page numbers and coordinates refer to the road atlas
(O) Site/address located off the map. Coordinates are also given for places that are not marked on the road atlas
(U A1) Coordinates for the map of Havana inside the back cover

(*A–B 2–3)* refers to the removable pull-out map
(*a–b 2–3)* refers to the additional inset map on the pull-out map

INSIDE FRONT COVER:
The best Highlights

INSIDE BACK COVER:
Map of Havana

The best MARCO POLO Insider Tips

Our top 15 Insider Tips

INSIDER TIP Sweet delights

An Austrian confectioner named Josef conjures up the finest Austrian pastries and dishes for artists, intellectuals and other guests at his *Casa Austria* in Camagüey → **p. 65**

INSIDER TIP Excellent guide

Explore the sights and sounds of the small eastern town of *Banes* with the *historiador* (a mixture between historian and storyteller) Luis Rafael Quiñones → **p. 79**

INSIDER TIP Treetop dining

Dine on platforms amongst the branches while enjoying the fantastic view – at the *Balcón del Valle* restaurant in Viñales → **p. 55**

INSIDER TIP In salon style

Eating at the *Museo Quince Catorce* restaurant (the name translates as Museum 1514) is like dining in a colonial museum: you'll be treated to a fine-dining experience and fantastic cuisine at this location in Trinidad → **p. 72**

INSIDER TIP All is perfect

Enjoy the fantastic view of the bay, the imaginative cuisine and top service – at the *Finca del Mar* in Cienfuegos, everything is perfect → **p. 67**

INSIDER TIP Stalking

On a walk to the mountain ridge *Loma de Piedra* in the *Humboldt National Park* near Baracoa you'll have a good chance of spotting the todi and tocororo (photo right) → **p. 78**

INSIDER TIP Church with a heart of gold

Pirates once dreamed about this fine specimen – the gilded altar of the *Catedral de San Juan Bautista,* one of the oldest on Cuba → **p. 71**

INSIDER TIP Hideaway

In a cosy corner close to the Malecón promenade in Havana, the star chef of the *Ivan Chefs Justo* treats his fans to fantastic culinary delights → **p. 40**

INSIDER TIP Be happy

As the saying goes at the *Casa del Cacao* cocoa shop in Baracoa "If you are sad... eat chocolate!" And where else but here! Treats include hot chocolate, chocolate ice cream or hot chocolate with rum → **p. 77**

INSIDER TIP A pig's ear? No way!

There is nothing cleaner than the water in the *Caleta Buena* natural basins near Playa Girón in the legendary Pig's Bay (photo left) → **p. 61**

INSIDER TIP St. Pauli in Santiago

The cheap and cheerful establishment, *St. Pauli,* plays homage to the cult German football club from Hamburg and has turned into a cult destination itself → **p. 84**

INSIDER TIP Dancing for a good cause

Tourism today: Book tickets for a *ballet performance* and you will be supporting a children's aid organisation in Camagüey → **p. 64**

INSIDER TIP Breezy observation post

Windswept hill with excellent restaurant: From the *Mirador La Gobernadora* you have excellent views over Guantánamo Bay with its infamous US naval base and detention camp → **p. 77**

INSIDER TIP Behind the Capitol

"Hemingway would have liked it here" is how the owners of *Sia Kava* in Havana promote their café – and the old man would have been left to his writing here → **p. 41**

INSIDER TIP Cuban nostalgia

Grab yourself a piece of "old" Cuba: The *Memories* bric-a-brac shop in Havana sells antique posters, books and newspapers on Cuba as well as car plaques and much more besides → **p. 40**

BEST OF...

FOR FREE

● *The people's stage*
The best place to sit back and enjoy the sunset is on the little wall bordering the *Malecón* of Havana – 3 miles long and running along the sea: this meeting place with the city skyline as backdrop provides excellent "urban theatre" – no ticket required (photo) → p. 33

● *Rhythms & rituals*
Drum roll in the *Callejón de Hamel:* on a Sunday, this small alleyway of Havana-Centro gives itself over to dance, worship of African deities and to offering tourists all kinds of magic stuff. A free spectacle, not only for Santería fans! → p. 36

● *Skateboarder show*
Watch in awe as cool Havana youngsters fly around the *skate park in Vedado* at record speeds, performing breakneck moves on their boards; the skateboarders enjoy the attraction of passers-by → p. 18

● *Open-air concert*
Every evening from 10pm a big open-air music extravaganza of Cuban bands is staged on the *Escalinata* in Trinidad – and everybody is invited. Only the drinks at the bar have to be paid → p. 67

● *One peso paradise for the children*
Merry-go-rounds, slides, swings and more to delight every child at the pleasure park *Isla del Coco* in Havana. Admission costs just one peso – that's around 2 pence... → p. 108

● *Che forever*
Pay your respects to the philosopher of the "New Man": thousands of Che fans from all over the world have already visited his last place of rest, the *Museo Memorial del Ernesto Che Guevara* in Santa Clara – and it's free to boot. This is surely what the man himself would have wanted... → p. 70

●●●●● Dots in guidebook refer to "Best of..." tips

● *Divine equation*
Every Christian saint has its African goddess equivalent! Oshun is syncretised with the patron saint
of Cuba, Our Lady of Charity, and because the
orisha spirit is yellow, many Cubans bring
sunflowers to her pilgrimage site → **p. 86**

● *Taste of Cuba*
Cool like the crushed ice, the soda water
and the fresh mint, sweet as Cuban sugar and enchanting like light Cuban rum,
that's what a real mojito should taste like.
The top place to sample one is Havana's *La
Bodeguita del Medio* → **p. 41**

● *Houses of song*
Clear the stage for son, salsa, bolero or trova – in
Cuba, the *casas de la trova* ("song houses") are places
of worship, where people show reverence when dancing or
just listening to the musicians. One with a particularly good ambience
is in Santiago de Cuba → **p. 84**

● *Holy smoke*
Cuba boasts the world's best tobacco plantations, and the aroma of a
true "Havana" sets cigar lovers on the path to ecstasy. Visit the factories of *Partagás* in Havana or *Donatién* in Pinar del Río to watch how
they are made (photo) → **p. 41, 52**

● *Revolution in the museum*
Cuba wouldn't be the same without its *revolutionary museums*. In Santa Clara, Santiago de Cuba and Havana in particular, the government
honours its heroes with museums and memorials. → **p. 37, 70, 83**

● *The real national anthem*
There can't be many who don't know *Guantanamera,* Cuba's world-famous ballad? The lyrics by national hero José Martí honour a peasant
woman from *Guantánamo;* Fernández Díaz set them to music → **p. 77**

● *Street festivals*
Music for the masses has a tradition in Cuba. The entire village gath-
ers together for street dances or a Sunday concert such as in *Remedios* → **p. 71**

ONLY ON

BEST OF...

● *Papa's retreat*
A visit to "Papa" Hemingway's former *Finca La Vigía* is travelling back in time – could there have been a better place to write than that? In Hemingway's time, the finca was not yet situated between main roads like today (photo) → **p. 48**

● *Trip into the underworld*
Down in the cave, the weather outside doesn't matter: the vaults and corridors of the *Cuevas de Bellamar* in Matanzas form an intricate subterranean system. The intrepid grab a pit lamp and explore unlit corners → **p. 110**

● *Warehouse shopping*
Rest assured, boredom will never set in at the undercover *Feria Antiguos Almacenes Nave San José* in Havana, an enormous market hall where you can find all kinds of souvenirs and enjoy a coffee → **p. 36**

● *Worlds of faith*
The confusing and disturbing world of the Cuban Santería and secret societies is excellently displayed in the *Museo Histórico de Guanabacoa*. For all the explanations, the exhibits speak their own language → **p. 48**

● *Chandeliers and mahogany*
Noblesse oblige... to lead an upper-crust lifestyle – the extent of which can be admired in the former Palacio Brunet, today's *Museo Romántico* in Trinidad → **p. 72**

● *Wax figures*
Cuban's only *wax works (Museo de Cera)* is located a bit off the beaten track, but if you're in Bayamo, don't miss saying hello to life-size likenesses of Benny Moré, Compay Segundo and Polo Montañez → **p. 86**

RAIN

RELAX AND CHILL OUT
Take it easy and spoil yourself

● *Sitting comfortably?*
Sometimes only an open-top Chrysler Bel Air with soft leather seating will do. This kind of 1950s cruiser picks up guests for relaxing tours of the city in Havana → **p. 34**

● *Serious pampering*
"Sauna, sensual showers, sun" is the promise made to spa fans by the *Paradisus Río de Oro & Spa* resort on Playa Esmeralda (photo) → **p. 80**

● *Full steam ahead*
Lean back and enjoy the view: daily at 9.30am the *tren de vapor* steam train leaves the Estación de Toro in Trinidad to head into the valley of the sugar mills (Valle de los Ingenios) and back → **p. 72**

● *Laid-back ferry cruise*
Take the leisurely "Lancha" ferry ride over the *Bahia de Habana* to Regla and soak in the fantastic views of the harbour → **p. 36**

● *Exclusive baths*
Pampering and relaxation at the *Acuavida Spa Talaso* on Cayo Coco. This spa offers all kinds of treatments including mud and chocolate packs to be enjoyed on its cliffside outdoor terraces → **p. 69**

● *Above the rooftops*
The best bit about the historic *Hotel Raquel* is the roof terrace. All we need now is a *cafecito* – or is it time already for a mojito? *The* place to lean back and enjoy Havana's rooftop landscape → **p. 42**

● *Paseo colonial: two-horse power*
The horses are harnessed, the coachman is sitting on his box: your job is to lean back, and you're away! In Old Havana it's easy to find a gentle carriage drive: they wait for passengers at Parque Central → **p. 43**

INTRODUCTION

DISCOVER CUBA!

To set things straight from the start: The situation in Cuba has not really changed. It remains the only Communist country in the west and the U.S. embargo still exists (even if the sanctions have been relaxed over the years); the revolutionaries of the past are ever present in this country still under the grip of poverty – despite the numerous economic reforms introduced by President Raúl Castro, for example to allow the establishment of small businesses and entrepreneurs. Although the socialist state is far more *diverse than it once was* its fragility is quickly evident after economic setbacks such as the devastating effects of Hurricane Irma. And crisis after crisis, the heroes of the day are the Cubans themselves: they are *masters in survival* who love their tropical paradise with all their heart!

Cuba has always been "special": the first to fall in love with the island's beauty was of course Columbus soon followed by the Spaniards who filled up their *galleons with treasures* in Cuba before heading back to Spain. Cuba also laid claim to being the world's largest producer of sugar. During alcohol and gambling prohibition in the USA, the island also became a haven for gamblers and hedonists: Cuba was *America's cesspit of corruption*.

It was however the revolution that finally gave Cuba its myth-like status as bearded young men in military attire led by Fidel Castro and his brother Raúl, Camilo Cienfuegos and Ernesto "Che" Guevara ousted the then dictator Fulgencio Batista *to establish their own, more equal society*. The rich were expropriated of their possessions and their wealth was "socialised", education and medical care became free for everyone while sexism and racism were banished. The world looked on while this revolution changed the face of Latin America. When the former U.S. President Barack Obama restored diplomatic relations following half a century of cold war between Cuba and USA, he created loopholes in the U.S. embargo, by loosening travel policies for students or aid organisations for urgently needed financial know-how and for Internet giants from the USA. Al-

though his predecessor Donald Trump has reinforced some of the business and travel restrictions loosened by the Obama Administration, he has left many of the changes – mainly for financial interests – in place. Cuba continues to signal that it is *ready for talks*. Only one subject is not open for discussion: nobody is prepared to be dictated to by the USA as this would be a betrayal of the revolution. Cuba's economy continues to struggle. The country is still suffering from decades of mismanagement under socialist rule. Some believe this to be a blessing in disguise though: Havana's *morbid charm* would not be the same without the withering neglect of its patchwork, half-deserted buildings; or the countryside if high-tech combine-harvesters were to replace the age-old oxen for ploughing the fields. If it's your first time in

A wind of change in the country

1000 BC – AD 1000
Arawak Indians arrive

1492
Columbus takes possession of Cuba for the Spanish crown

1553
Havana becomes capital and the main shipyard for New Spain

1762
England conquers Havana. Shortly after, Cuba is swapped for Spanish Florida

1789–1820
Flow of refugees from Haiti. Cuba becomes the largest exporter of sugar

Colonial charm beneath palm trees: Trinidad

Cuba, you will first be taken aback by the decaying houses, burst water pipes or power cuts in Havana; all a reminder of the country's backwardness. Look closer though and you'll notice how *ingenious the Cubans are* and how they have learnt to improvise and turn a crisis into an opportunity. And you'll maybe come to the conclusion that the country is, for Cuban standards, in an excellent state.

Public spirit and a will to survive

You can almost *feel the unity* between the country and its people on Cuba. If you want to experience this feeling, you will have to take a look beyond your luxury all-inclusive hotel accommodation in Varadero, on the Cayería del Norte, Jardines del Rey or the Holguín province and *explore the island.* Simply get out and take a

1868–78
First War of Independence against Spain

1895–98
Second War of Independence; leading after US intervention to dependence on the USA

1902
Cuba becomes a republic

1902–58
Sugar export boom in the World War I. US-controlled puppet presidents, the last of whom was dictator F. Batista

1953–59
Victory of the revolution under Fidel Castro – after time spent in prison and years of exile in Mexico

horse-drawn carriage, a bicycle taxi or a taxi. But don't worry about your safety: Cuba is one of the *safest places in Latin America.* For longer excursions around the island, you have the choice between the fast *Viazul* buses, slow trains or a hire car. Traffic on Cuba is orderly (due to the many speed checks) and if you are vigilant and have some knowledge of Spanish, travelling around the island is both safe and

> **Waterfalls, limestone mountains, royal palms and magnificent beaches**

easy. You will be treated to *a vast and diverse Caribbean landscape*, rich in green plains, mountains, white coral beaches and offshore islands. The island's west, in Viñales, is dominated by the tobacco red earth in between the famous *mogotes,* the 160 to 140 million year old eroded limestone mountains. They are enormous rocks originating long before the Lesser Antilles and have been declared a Unesco world heritage site. They are an image of *mystical beauty*, especially to hikers early in the morning when surrounded by mist. The mogotes are part of the Sierra de los Órganos where the earliest rocks of the Caribbean were found. Together with five other mountainous islands, they rose from the sea in Miocene (24 to 5 million years ago), connected in parts with Hispaniola and Jamaica.

The present long, narrow shape of the island has existed for just 7 million years and stretches 1250 km/777 miles from east to west, at just 31 km/19miles wide at its narrowest point – 7 million years ago with its vast green plains between mountain ranges. The Cuban poet Nicolás Guillén (1902–89) compared the island's shape to a crocodile lying laughing on his back. Indeed, the crocodile is a native animal on Cuba and the Cuban crocodile is a species found only in Cuba. It lives in the Ciénaga de Zapata, the *largest swamp region in the Caribbean* and one of Cuba's seven national parks to be declared as a biosphere reserve. Nature enthusiasts can explore the nature reserves with guides organised by the information centres on the island (or book in advance with an agency offering tour guides in your own language). The country's most diverse national park was named after the famous German explorer *Alexander von Humboldt.* It spreads out behind the small and quiet town of Baracoa (founded in 1511) where the Spaniards founded their first colonial government. Terracotta roofs, windows with grilles, high wooden doors – many of Cuba's towns and cities are still dominated by *early Colonial architecture,* espe-

1960
The US economic embargo starts to kick in; the USSR becomes trading partner number one

1991–94
Economic crisis after the collapse of the USSR. A tourist infrastructure is set up

2008
After 49 years as head of state, a very sick Fidel Castro transfers the office to his brother Raúl.

2015–17
Cuba and the USA restore diplomatic relations in 2015 with relaxations in the embargo; Fidel Castro dies at the age of 90 in 2016; in 2017 Hurricane Irma eradicates the northern coast

Smaller ones available for export: XXL cigar made in Cuba

cially the six oldest cities: Bayamo (founded 1512), Remedios, Sancti Spíritus and Trinidad (in 1514) as well as the predecessor to Baracoa as the capital city, Santiago de Cuba (1515) and of course Havana (1519). Pretentious palaces from the late colonial period can be seen in cities such as Holguín or Matanzas where Spanish sugar barons and their slaves amounted a *vast wealth* from sugar while the rest of America had long since been independent.

Colonial grandeur with a living history

The crowned highlight among all of Cuba's cities is of course *Havana*, a capital city which has been the inspiration for many books and songs over the centuries: whether for its coastal location where the sea sprays salt over the capital, or for its splendid architecture from various periods, or for its old houses which tell the most amazing stories, calle for calle, avenida for avenida. For example of the racketeer and pimp Alberto Yarini y Ponce de Léon, named "El Rey" (the King), who was born into an elite Havana family and lived with his six wives in the Calle Paula no. 96, of famous dancers such as Josefine Baker, of Mafiosi such as Meyer Lansky and of course the "Papa" himself, Ernest Hemingway. These old stories are slowly resurging, dug out by Cuban writers such as Leonardo Padura. Their tales reveal another history behind the now restored streets of Havana — and dispel the untruths of a *revolution wise with age*.

WHAT'S HOT

1 Breakneck speeds

Skateboarding The skateboarders at the ● Malecón skate park *(corner of Calle A, in front of the Galerías de Paseo)* race around the track at hair-raising speeds, performing the craziest stunts and landing safely (well mostly). A non-profit organisation based in Washington has funded the project for years by providing skateboards. The YouTube film "Ritual" brought international fame to the park and the number of skateboarders in Havana has grown to over a thousand. A second park was also opened in 2017 on the corner of Paseo/Calle 31.

White wedding days 2

Church ceremonies Not complete without all the special trimmings, including flower arrangements, decorated horse-drawn carriages or polished vintage cars. Ever since more recent Popes have visited Cuba and the places of worship have re-opened their doors, young couples seem intent on getting married in church, a ceremony which was once denied to their mothers and fathers. Afterwards, they make sure to seek the blessing of the Orishas, the Afro-Cuban Gods... By the way: most newlyweds love to have their photo taken by onlookers!

3 Voicing opinion

Blogging Cubans refuse to keep quiet despite the controversy surrounding the freedom of the press in Cuba. Those who want to be heard today start a blog, to express their love for their country and to share their thoughts with other internet users; comments are always welcome. The websites are homemade in wordpress and then posted on the network. There is an alphabetic list of blogs available at *blogscubanos.wordpress.com* to limit your search.

On the move

Collective mobility Admittedly, travelling around the countryside can still be difficult in Cuba. However in the cities the *carros colectivos* or *taxis colectivos* have improved transportation so much so that there would be a public outcry if they were to be banned again. Most of these rattling old taxis are vintage American old-timers, kept lovingly in service by their owners. The taxi plates are usually stuck in unorthodox places on the car and they travel for cheap peso prices on fixed routes known to the Cubans. It goes without saying that the more passengers, the more lucrative business is for the taxi driver, which is why you often see four squeezed onto the back seat and two at the front. And although tourists are technically not allowed to take public transportation, taxi drivers will make an exception if you are prepared to pay a bit more and preferably in CUC.

4

Art from nothing

5

Upcycling Making a virtue out of necessity. Lucía Fernández for one turns trash into sculptures. And very successfully at that: her works even made it onto the runway of the *Art and Style Fashion* show in Havana. The *Guerra de la Paz* group *(www.guerradelapaz.com)* creates impressive sculptures from old clothing. Their works in bonsai or snake shapes enjoy international success. In Angel Ramírez' works, old materials finish up on the walls as two-dimensional paintings *(www.amramirez.com) (photo)*. The *Servando* gallery *(C/ 23 1151/corner of C/10 | Vedado | Havana)* supports local artists.

IN A NUTSHELL

UNIFORMS FOR SCHOOL ONLY

Eccentric, musical, temperamental, feisty and brash – are the Cubans really like their stereotypes portray them? One thing is clear: the Cubans (11.2 million in total) don't like to be put in boxes. The revolution has inspired them to become self-confident individuals whose social status is not dictated by the colour of their skin or where they come from. This belief is underpinned by the country's policy of free education for all, and not least by the obligatory school uniform worn by all pupils. It therefore might appear to go against the grain to call someone with a slightly Asian appearance (maybe because his ancestors were from Asia) a *Chino* or a national park ranger with Indian heritage an *Indio*. However nobody takes offense. Why would they? These nicknames have absolutely no discriminatory influence on a person's social standing.

(INTER)NATIONAL HERO

His Cuban wife and mother of his four children, Aleida March, described him in her book "Evocación" (memories) as a loyal and integral man while his brother Juan Martín Guevara remembered him as "stubborn with a thirst for knowledge" and as a "prankster and mocker": Ernesto "Che" Guevara was a young doctor from an affluent Argentine family who joined Fidel Castro's movement in Mexico, secured the victory of the Cuban revolution in Santa Clara and then

From architecture to economy: what new-comers should know in order to see beyond Cuba's tropical façade

chose the life of a revolutionary rather than taking up a minister's post in Cuba. Although Che died over 50 years ago, many youngsters in Cuba strive to emulate him. Why? Was it his eternal dream to create the consciousness of a "new man" driven by moral rather than material incentives? His early death (1967) in Bolivia turned him into a quintessential icon; his dream became a promise of salvation and was spared the scrutiny of reality. And people from around the world, in Japan, China, Brazil or the UK, come to visit his grave in Santa Clara to thank him.

LEGACY OF AN EXPLORER

Considered to be the "second discoverer of Cuba", the German naturalist and botanist Alexander von Humboldt visited Cuba in 1800 and 1801. Did he also spot the tiny bee hummingbird (5 cm/0.39 in), the colibri zunzunito, and the 9.6 mm/0.003 in Monte Iberia eleuth (type of frog) with its striking yellow and black stripes? Probably. This inquisitive explorer left no stone unturned during his natural history travels. Even today, naturalists in Latin America hold Alexander von Humboldt in high esteem, treating him like a superstar. Cuba named its largest and most unspoilt of its 14 national parks after him, the *Parque Nacional Alejandro de Humboldt*. This park is also home to the bee hummingbird, now identified as the world's smallest bird, and the miniature frog. The endemic Santa María boa constrictor, which can attain up to 6 m/20 ft in length, can also be found in the tropical undergrowth as well as the island's national bird, the colourful tocororo, can be heard singing in the trees. Cuba's national flower is the sweet-smelling mariposa lily while the national tree is unsurprisingly the toweringly high palma real (the royal palm) which grows all over the island. The island is home to a plethora of flora and fauna such as flamingos, crocodiles and coral reefs teeming with shoals of fish – let your *guía* (guide) take you to the right spots in the (underwater) parks. Information at: *www.turnatcuba.com*

INSIDER'S PERSPECTIVE

To understand how Cubans tick, it's worth delving into Cuban literature. Don't worry though: the works of the most famous writers are available in English, for example those by Leonardo Padura (*1955) whose crime novels are set in pre-revolutionary Cuba. Another popular author is Zoé Valdés (*1959). Her book "La nada cotidiana" (English: Yocandra in the Paradise of Nada) focuses on the difficulties living under the Cuban regime. Miguel Barnet (*1940) is another successful novelist best known for his books "Cimarrón" (English: "Biography of a Runaway Slave") and "Everybody Dreams about Cuba". Those looking to understand the revolution should read the works of José Martí (1853–95), Cuba's most famous writer. Affected by political repression early on, he left an extensive oeuvre of letters, speeches, essays and collections of poetry when he died at a young age during the struggle to liberate Cuba. To really get to grips with Cuba, Alejo Carpentier's (1904–80) novel "My Havana" or Guillermo Cabrera Infante's (1929–2005) book "Three Trapped Tigers" are must-reads which both shed a different light on Cuba. Cuba's national poet is Nicolás Guillen (1902–1989), a mulatto born in Camagüey with a profound sense of humour.

CUBAN RHYTHMS AROUND THE WORLD

Its calming rhythm and melancholic melody are unmistakable, conjuring up images of couples dancing in a tight embrace as if lost together in another time and place. "Dos gardenias para ti..." or "two gardenias for you" is a famous bolero interpreted by many artists, but none as fervently as Ibrahim Ferrer (1927–2005), the ageing star of the international film hit "Buena Vista Social Club" by Ry Cooder and Wim Wenders. Ferrer was born in Santiago de Cuba, the city Cuba has to thank for its captivating music. Its music tradition dates to the start of the 19th century when Santiago (like New Orleans) became the landing point for refugees from the French neighbouring colony of Sainte Domingue, later Haiti. Among these refugees were the forefathers of the bolero; ballad singers *(charangas)* who moved around the country earning their living by singing and playing the guitar. The French white upper class brought the French contra dance *danzón* with them while their African slaves introduced the *tumba francesa*. These genres were then experimentally amalgamated with the existing rhythms such as the Spanish flamenco to create the *rumba* and the *son*. Son first captivated Havana and then spread to the clubs in New York and around the world. And while the dance evolved into the *salsa* in New York, the revolution in Cuba called a halt to any further interpretation, denouncing this type of music as decadent. It was replaced with political songs *(Nueva Trova)* or folk music such as "Guantanamera" (text by José Martí). While the danzón and rumba have since been added to UNESCO's list of intangible heritages, today the Cuban youth rebel against the nostalgic Cuban sounds of the Buena Vista Social Club (played in tourist bars) with their exciting mixture of reggae, hip-hop and merengue. A new vibrant and sensual jazz scene is also establishing itself in the city clubs.

YO SOY FIDEL

In 2016 the death of Fidel Castro, the father of the Cuban revolution and *comandante en jefe* from 1959 to 2008, was accompanied by days of deep national mourning. The grief was felt throughout the country despite the growing dissatisfaction caused by the country's economic problems and his biting condemnation of any critics to the regime. Many Cubans cried "Murió mi segundo padre!" – "It's the death of my second father", particularly those who could remember the poverty-stricken Cuba of their childhood, the damp wooden and clay-floored huts in the mountains and the illness and hunger. It took Fidel Castro's revolution to bring an end to these miserable conditions and to introduce literacy programs and free open universities for all. Although many Cubans have emigrated over the years and many others wish for political change, the majority it seems is grateful

to their patriarch for returning social justice to the country. For them, Fidel Castro was not a dictator but their saviour and protector. They cry out "Yo soy Fidel" – "I am Fidel", a saying written in graffiti all over the country.

Heart-felt grief: book of condolences for Fidel Castro

UNCERTAIN FUTURE

Although Cuba is one of the last surviving communist countries, the question is for how long still? Nobody knows what changes the only legal party in Cuba, the Partido Comunista de Cuba (PCC), have in mind once Raúl Castro steps down from power. He announced at the last party conference that he would not be standing for presidency in 2018. The days of the governing revolutionaries seem numbered but who and what will replace them? A potential candidate is Castro's young vice-president, the smart Miguel Mario Díaz-Canel Bermúdez (born 1960). But will there be further reforms, or even a move towards democracy? The voting age is 16 in Cuba and a secret ballot system was introduced in 1992 allowing citizens to vote for or against candidates on the electoral list for the National Assembly *(Asamblea Nacional)*. This reduced the original number of 612 delegates who in turn elect the members of the State and Ministry Council. One of the main challenges facing Raúl Castro's successor will be to restore the diplomatic relations negotiated between Castro and Obama so far that the economic embargo against Cuba can finally be lifted without relinquishing Cuba's national independence. Not an easy task, especially with the U.S. President Donald Trump as a sparring partner.

HEMINGWAY AND THE SEA

The fishermen of Cojímar were particularly devoted to him. He often joined them to share the catch of the day, drink at the bar *La Terraza* and in turn they gave him the affectionate nickname "papa": Ernest Hemingway (1899–1961), the only U.S. citizen who the Cubans hold in loving and lasting memory. After his suicide, the fishermen of Cojímar melted down ship propellers into a monument which they erected at the port. It was maybe their way of thanking Hemingway for his literary homage to them in his book "The Old Man and the Sea" for which he won the Nobel Prize for Literature in 1959. Or maybe it was simply a sign that they had lost a good friend. Hemingway had apparently seen something in them which he hadn't witnessed before as a war reporter in Europe or big game hunter in Africa: the daily fight for survival of normal folk. Nobody describes their endless hope of a great catch, their struggle and their surrendering to fate quiet so poignantly and touchingly as Hemingway does.

FOR BOOKWORMS & FILM BUFFS

Telex from Cuba – The novel (2008) by Rachel Kushner narrates the Cuban revolution from the perspective of executive anglo-expatriates living and working in Cuba at this time

My Brother Che – The book (2017) written by Juan Martín Guevara, the fifteen year younger brother of Che Guevara for all those who want to learn more about this revolutionary

7 Days in Havana – Set in Havana during one week and allotting one day to each character, seven film directors, among them Benicio Del Toro, tell their stories from Cuba (2013)

Fast and Furious 8 – The first Hollywood production to be filmed in Cuba after the relaxation of the U.S. embargo (2017). Great racing car scenes with an old Cuban car revamped into a veritable rocket!

THE CRUX WITH CUP AND CUC

Over 70 percent of state-employed Cubans earn an average of 824 CUP a month, that's approximately 33 US $. Who can survive off that, you may ask? which is pegged to the U.S. dollar. Cubans can exchange the U.S. based currency for pesos at exchange offices, but at an exchange rate of 1:24 you get little for your money. Those who work in tourism, for example suitcase carriers,

Shopping on farmers' markets with Cuban pesos (CUP): garlic in Camagüey, for example

Cubans can. Why? Because almost everything they need is subsidised by the state and is either extremely cheap or free: the cost of rent, electricity, water, gas, telephone and bus travel is extremely cheap. Cubans are also entitled to free education as well as free healthcare. The *libreta*, the food card (similar to a rations book), provides a basic supply of food. The peso wage covers a few purchases at the farmers' markets or in the workshops. But that's about it.

Consumer items are regarded as luxuries and not essential in this anti-capitalistic system. Anyone intent on buying a mobile phone or TV has to deal in *Peso Convertible,* the CUC, the value of hotel maids or tourist guides are the luckier ones as CUCs flow like milk and honey in this sector. Or Cubans with relatives in the USA or Spain who regularly send dollars or euros. The winners are those who have a spare room to let *(casas particulares)* or a restaurant *(paladar)*. While some Cubans are making themselves rich (despite the country's high taxes), unluckier ones without relatives abroad and no access to tourists can only dream of consumer goods. The gap is growing between the rich and poor, which creates envy and threatens to topple the social benefits of the revolution.

FOOD & DRINK

A lime, six fresh mint leaves, a teaspoon of sugar, two centilitres of rum, soda water, garnished with one twig of mint – and you have your Cuban national drink, the *mojito*. Or how about the drink that Ernest Hemingway is said to have loved: a light-green daiquirí from sugar-cane syrup, rum and lime juice?

Or then again maybe you prefer a Mary Pickford, a Havana special, a canchanchara or, last not least, a *Cuba libre*? Add the ambience of a bar from Havana's famously infamous 1920s and 1930s, when US mafiosi Al Capone and Meyer Lansky were regulars here, most of all though Hemingway, who was not averse to the odd drink or ten. In a way, the *cocktail bars* still live off the legendary Prohibition era between 1920 and 1933, when alcohol production and consumption was banned in the US. At the time, Cuba was the only legal fuel stop for drinkers and the hub of alcohol sales, with a tropical location to boot. Hemingway's favourite bar, *El Floridita*, and *La Bodeguita del Medio* are a must when visiting Havana. Whether *Cuba libre, mojito* or *daiquirí:* the mixing base is **white rum** which has matured for five or more years in oak casks. With increasing age it displays a darker colour and is called *añejo*. Rum is enjoyed neat *(ron seco)* or on the rocks *(ron con hielo)*. The world's most famous rum was originally from Cuba: Bacardí. The *Havana Club*, where US businessmen met and the **Bacardí distilling dynasty** poured rum for its guests, has remained a legend. While

Alongside cocktails, fish and shellfish, Cuban cuisine is enriched by rustic fare using fresh produce from the farmers' markets

the Bacardís fled to Puerto Rico following the revolution, Cuba still looks after the heritage of its most famous family of exiles. The name "Havana Club" was immortalised in the rum of revolutionary Cuba.

Beer drinkers can choose between several brands. A refreshing lager-style beer is *Cristal* for example. Coffee drinkers should try the *café cubano*, which is served black with sugar in small cups. *Guarapo* is the name for cloudy, slightly sweet juice from the **sugar cane**, re-

freshing despite its sweetness. A special treat are the **freshly squeezed juices** of sun-ripened tropical fruit such as *piñas* (pineapple), mangos, papayas, guavas, lemons or limes, oranges and grapefruit. The subject of food was long overshadowed by the difficult supply situation. Occasionally you can still feel this. So don't be too surprised when restaurants only have a small selection of dishes or others mentioned on the menu are unavailable "at the moment". It's a different situation in the **private**

LOCAL SPECIALITIES

ajiaco bayamés – stew from Bayamo with pork, maize-flour balls, cumin, tomatoes, onions, garlic, chilli and green bananas

arroz congrí (oriental) – rice with beans, garlic and bacon

arroz con pescado al ron – rice with fish soaked in rum, spiced with cloves and pepper

bacalao con plátano – codfish with cooked green banana

bocadito – warm filled bread roll

calamares – octopus rings

carne asada – seared meat, usually served with carrots, garlic, onions, leek and tomato and spiced with oregano and bay leaf

coquito blanco – sweet dessert made from coconut flesh

parrillada de pescado/carne – grill platter with various kinds of fish and meat

patas y panza guisado con arroz blanco – feet and belly of pork, cooked in water with allspice, salt, concentrated tomato puree and garlic; served with white rice

pato guisado – seared duck

picadillo a la Habanera – beef mince seared with onions, garlic, tomatoes and wine; it may also be crowned with fried eggs; eaten with white rice

pollo ahumado – savoury chicken, smoked before roasting

pollo frito a la criolla – chicken pieces marinated in orange, allspice, onions and garlic, and coated in flour before frying

potaje de frijoles negros – stew made from black beans with bacon, pieces of chorizo sausage and potatoes, garlic, concentrated tomato puree and onions, spiced with oregano, caraway and salt (photo right)

ropa vieja – "old clothes", beef cooked to a soft consistency and pulled into pieces, eaten in an aromatic sauce with white rice (photo left)

---

restaurants and *paladares* (as the first private restaurants were called; today the term is only used for smaller, more basic restaurants). Today, the hosts buy fresh produce from their own suppliers, **buy them on the markets daily** or buy ahead (imported goods) in Havana's markets for diplomats. By the way: if guests in a *casa particular* are offered half or full board, this is more than sheer politeness. The hosts pay high taxes for the right to feed their guests too. If you accept, you'll not only have satisfied your appetite, you'll also have helped your hosts to recoup the tax they paid. However, advise them of your wishes two hours ahead or at breakfast, as some ingredients have still to be got in specially.

Despite **Havana's ambitious new restaurant scene,** the food on most restaurant menus is traditional fare. A typical side dish is **rice with black beans**, *arroz moro.* In soups and as a side dish you'll often see boiled sweet potato *(boniato)*, ñame (yam root) or manioc root *(yuca)*. *Plátanos* (cooking bananas) are often served as deep-fried discs to go with fish or meat.

Soups form an integral part of traditional Cuban cuisine, which has strong Spanish and Moorish influences. You'll often find *sopa de ajo* on the menu, a simple yet delicious garlic soup and originally a Spanish classic.

The major delicacies of course include **seafood** such as crayfish, which is readily available, at least in the hotels. Fish is served boiled *(hervido)*, fried *(asado)*, oven-baked on pizza and in doughballs, or sometimes as *salpicón* (salad). Do be careful however in state-run restaurants on the motorways or beaches, as some of them get few guests. Like any other restaurant they have a licence to sell crayfish and other seafood, yet due to the scarcity of diners, the creatures are kept in freezers for longer – and on Cuba the electricity supply is as uncertain as the weather during the hurricane season: when the power fails, the content defrosts; when the electricity returns the content freezes again. This does not exactly create salubrious conditions for consumption. **Langoustines are usually extremely fresh and affordable when served in private restaurants.** However they

are prepared to perfection (so that the meat remains tender) more in the higher-end restaurants.

On Cuba, bad stomach bugs are usually down to rotten seafood, and are caused less often by contaminated **water**. Still, don't forget to ask for *agua sana* (clean

Refreshing: Cuba's national drink, the Mojito

water) when ordering drinks with water, and avoid ice cubes and salads.

If you're dining at one of the **better restaurants**, bear in mind that guests wait at the entrance for the waiter to lead them to a free table. There's usually no need to make a reservation.

SHOPPING

Apart from the classics – cigars, rum or CDs with hot Cuban rhythms – the capital behind the production of many souvenirs in Cuba is the imagination. Improvisation with the materials available has to replace large-scale industrial production. There is certainly no lack of ideas. On the markets, typically Cuban vintage cars manufactured from colourful used drinks cans are amongst the bestsellers. Craft artists outdo each other in the creative use of raw materials such as wood, shells, sisal or fabric, turning them into Creole dolls, garden or children's furniture and jewellery in the most outlandish variations. There is plenty of crochet work, straw hats and bags, reproductions of old Spanish sailing ships in model size. The state, for its part, raided the archives to offer Che Guevara fans the world over likenesses of the glorified revolutionary on t-shirts and postcards, in coffee-table books, on bookends and even on trouser braces.

Usually you can count on the following opening times: shops *Mon–Sat 10/11am–7.30pm*, tourist shops *daily 9am–9pm*, banks *Mon–Fri 8.30am–noon and 1.30–3pm*, bureaux de change *Mon–Sat 8am–6pm*, post offices *(correo) Mon–Fri 8am–6pm*. Shops in the Servi petrol stations are open around the clock.

ART

You'll find a great selection of art from Cuba in Havana, whether in the galleries of the Calle Obispo, in the *Taller experimental de Gráfica* at the Plaza de Catedral or at the *Mercado Artesanal* of the *Centro Cultural Antiguos Almacenes de Depósito San José* on the old harbour. You might be able to meet some of the artists in person on the markets. There is also an office *Registro Nacional de Bienes Culturales,* where an authorisation *(autorización)* for the export of art (required for paintings from 50 x 50 cm in size) is stamped. Extra costs: bei nicht registrierten Künstlern 2–3 CUC, bei registrierten 5 CUC.

CIGARS

The best opportunity for buying real Havanas is a visit to one of the many cigar factories *(fábricas de tabaco)*, where you may watch the *tabaqueros* at work. Maybe you'll catch one of the readers who entertain the workers by reading out stories! Be careful with special offers

Cuba is a great territory for souvenir hunters: art objects, fine Havana cigars, Cuban rum, music for connoisseurs

on the street: they are nearly always fake versions of the globally famous brands such as Cohiba, Romeo y Julieta or Montecristo. Remember that to export more than 50 cigars you need the receipts from the shop in both original and copy (for the customs official); the cigars also have to be in their original packaging and bear the new holographic stamp.

MUSIC

If you want to take home Cuban rhythms, you won't have to look far. Whether in cafés, bars or in a Casa de la Trova: wherever bands play, they'll sell CDs with their music, signed by the artists on request. In terms of audio quality, these CDs are hardly ever first choice. The discs produced at the state-run Egrem studios have much better sound quality and are on offer in any souvenir shop. The selection is particularly good in the ARTEX shops. Musicians currently producing hits

include Los Van Van and Manolito (salsa) and Gente de a Zona (reggaeton). More information on the artists (with online music): *www.egrem.com*.

RUM

Whether "Ron Mulata", "Ron Varadero", "Ron Santiago de Cuba", "Ron Caney" *(www.roncaney.it/en)* or "Havana Club" *(www.havana-club.com):* Rum from the sugar island of Cuba is world-famous for its top quality. Today, Havana Club is the best-known Cuban brand in the world. You can get Havana Club in all hotel shops and souvenir shops. Aged for three years and white, it is the essential basis for various Cuban cocktails. The wonderfully golden-brown shimmering *Gran Reserva* is matured for several years in wooden barrels. Five and seven-year-old Gran Reserva brands are the ones you're most likely to see for sale. They are enjoyed neat or with ice, like a good whisky.

HAVANA

MAP INSIDE THE BACK COVER (129 E–F2) (**D2**) **"In Havana, my friend, anything goes, as long as you're not a bore". This is what folk wisdom has to say about life in Cuba's capital city.**

This assessment was never so timely as now, as a variety of small businesses show the slow-moving socialist state enterprises what is possible. Today, the streets are lined with small snack stalls selling hamburgers, hotdogs, pizza or fresh fruit juices; bike rickshaws offer their services as well as private taxis – and all this in Cuban peso prices for Cubans and at the correct rate of exchange in CUC. The whole thing seems a bit like a secret takeover of Havana by its citizens and free enterprise. The encouraging framework for this was created by city historian Eusebio Leal with his grand-scale restoration of the Old Town. This is far from being completed. It did however create a new Havana, which doesn't destroy itself anymore, a city that can be a player on the global stage again, in short a city that is in love with itself again after a long revolution-induced break. Little matter that the side streets of the Centro, for instance, still feature a number of towering scrap heaps and that crumbling façades of houses still bear witness to past disdain (and hurricane disasters). The biggest attraction of Havana (pop. 3 million) is the historic Old Town, which in 1982 was given World Heritage status by Unesco – the *Habana vieja,* with what was once the most important port

Bars, bodegas and bastion walls: no other Caribbean city charms visitors in the same way as the Unesco World Heritage city of Havana

connecting America to Europe. Typical for *Habana vieja* are narrow street canyons cutting through colonial, high baroque and neo-classical buildings. Stroll across squares with ancient cobbles where once the carriages of the fine folk used to park, past high double doors offering glimpses of aristocratic entrance halls or column-framed *patios*, step onto marble floors and run your hand over curved mahogany balustrades. The famous ● *Malecón* too, begins in the Old Town: turned longingly, you could say, towards the Straits of

Florida, it is the quay wall of the *enamorados*, lovers, and a show boulevard lined with columned façades, some of which have now been restored. Curving for miles along the coast towards the west, past the quarters of the Centro and the more recent Vedado, the Malecón ends at the tunnel to Quinta Avenida, the prestigious villa-lined street of Miramar, where many embassies are based. And in the east where the boulevard turns into Avenida del Puerto, you can branch off into the tunnel running under the narrowest

Greetings from Washington: the Capitol in Habana Centro

point of the harbour entrance. The tunnel leads into the Vía Monumental with its access road to the Complejo El Morro. The Vía Monumental then takes you to the Vía Blanca, whose exits fork off to the pretty beaches of the Playas del Este, and which then leads on to Varadero.

HABANA VIEJA/CENTRO

Alley after alley, square after square adorned with magnificent buildings from various eras – and music everywhere: ⭐ Habana vieja, the Old Town, is a vibrant monument to the centuries-long, almost uninterrupted rise of the city which was once one of the wealthiest in the Americas.

Every era left its trace. A tiny temple *(El Templete)* on the Plaza de Armas is testimony to 1519 when the *Villa San Cristóbal de La Habana,* founded by Diego Velázquez five years previously, was re-

located to its present site; fortress walls such as around the *Castillo de Real Fuerza* also testify to the port's prominence in 1535 when Spanish galleons from Central and South America were laden here with treasure. The aim was to defend vast riches, as shown by remains of the old

---

🏙 WHERE TO START?
Parque Central (U E2–3) *(🗺 e2–3):* This square is an international meeting place and tourist interface. In front of the *Hotel Parque Central* you'll find ● vintage taxis waiting to take you on a tour of the city for 50 CUC/hr; the stop for the good-value hop-on-hop-off sightseeing buses of Habana Bus Tour is in front of the *Hotel Inglaterra*, and if you need to book trips or rental cars, head for the arcade at nearby *Hotel Sevilla*. From Parque Central, it's only a few paces to the Old Town, the Prado and the Malecón.

city wall, a few scattered defensive walls or baluartes, and most of all the gigantic fortified complex of Morro-Cabaña. Everywhere you go, you'll meet signs of Cuba's former status as the world's biggest sugar producer: splendid palaces with wooden balconies, baronial portals or high wooden doors with imaginative *aldabas* (door knockers), leading on to arcaded patios and into rooms with coffered ceilings. Hotels and restaurants now reside in these renovated buildings; the old port buildings are also swarming with tourists sailing into the city on cruise ships and yachts. The Parque Central, the capitol and the old *Barrio Chino* already belong to Habana Centro. In Calle Galiano and Calle Rafael the quarter has its own shopping streets, and at the Malecón it looks its best: with neo-classical or art deco façades and high-ceilinged colonnades.

SIGHTSEEING

BAHÍA DE LA HABANA/AVENIDA DEL PUERTO (U E–F 1–2) (𝄜 e–f 1–2)

Don't panic: the only shootings still done here are with cameras and mobiles all pointed at the two enormous forts and a 17 m/55 ft high statue of Christ on the east bank and the dazzling city skyline with its harbour promenade, the Malecón, on the west bank. The east-bank fortifications are divided into the *Castillo de los Tres Reyes del Morro* built by the Spanish master builder Antonnelli (1589–1630) and the *Fortaleza de San Carlos de la Cabaña* (1763–1774). The canons are fired between 8pm and 9pm every evening at the *cañonazo* (canon ceremony) – the signal once given to close the city gates. Ancient weapons and artillery are also on exhibition in the grounds of the *Museo de Armas y Fortificaciones (daily 10am–10pm | admission 6 CUC, with cañonazo*

8 CUC). You can also see the world's largest cigars in the *Casa del Tabaco* and Che Guevara's first office in the *Comandancia del Che (Mon–Sat 10am–6pm, Sun 10am–1pm | admission 4 CUC)*.

Luxury liners dock along the west bank at the Avenida del Puerto which merges with the old part of the city. The cruise terminal *Sierra Maestra* lies directly across from the newly restored *Plaza de San Francisco de Asís* which welcomes visitors with the elegant *Café del Oriente (daily noon–midnight | tel. 78 60 66 86 | Expensive)*, the imposing Chamber of Commerce building *(Lonja del Comercio)* and the *San Francisco de Asis* monastery church (1608–1738) popular with wedding couples. Continue along this road to reach the *Museo Ron Havana Club (Av. del Puerto 262 | daily 9am–4pm | admission 7

★ Habana vieja
The Old Town: old alleyways taking on a new shine → p. 34

★ Avenida Quinta
Street of splendour in the embassy quarter → p. 43

★ Cabaret Tropicana
This world-famous dance revue is a must → p. 45

★ Nacional de Cuba
Nostalgic hotel reminiscence of a notorious past → p. 47

★ Playas del Este
Magnificent beaches near the capital → p. 48

★ Museo Hemingway
The Nobel Prize laureate lived and worked here → p. 48

MARCO POLO HIGHLIGHTS

CUC | www.havana-club.com) which gives an insight into rum production. It even houses a model of the *Central Azucarero La Esperanza* sugar factory including miniature trains and a glowing-red oven. Once you have passed the legendary port bar *Dos Hermanos,* you will spot the glass ferry house for the ● *Lancha de la Regla* ferry which ferries passengers between Habana Vieja and La Regla *(daily 7am–2pm, every 20 min. | 0.10 CUC).* Continue strolling along the promenade and you will soon reach the authentic pub *Cervecería* in the *Antigua Almacén de la Madera y*

bands drum for all they're worth, and Cubans dance themselves into a trance right there on the street. *Callejón de Hamel | betw. Aramburu/Hospital*

CALLE OBISPO (U E–F2) (*ID e–f2*)

A narrow corridor lane, where once there was only enough space for two horse-drawn carriages, is today a main interconnecting artery packed with a swaying throng of people drifting along the restored old centre of this Caribbean capital. Start your stroll along "Havana's Wall Street" (once the headquarters of the Na-

On Sundays there's dancing and singing on the Callejón del Hamel

el Tabaco and the large ● souvenir market *Feria Antiguos Almacenes Nave San José (daily 10am–6pm)* next door.

INSIDER TIP ► CALLEJÓN DE HAMEL ●
(U B–C2) (*ID b–c2*)
Worth a visit for the wall paintings in the alleyway, the small Santería shop stuffed full of cult objects, and the corner café. Traditionally, most Sundays *(noon–5pm),* a lively street party takes place (sadly, irregularly these days):

tional Bank in 1907) at the "home of daiquiri", the city's oldest bar and local of Ernest Hemingway *El Floridita (no. 557 | tel. 78 67 13 00 | www.floridita-cuba.com).* Its interior hasn't changed much since Hemingway's time and he is even there to greet you, albeit as a bronze sculpture. A few steps further on, *La Rosa boutique (between Villegas and Aguacate)* focuses on a more contemporary U.S. star, namely Jennifer Lopez whose collection of outfits can be purchased here. Diagonally opposite in the *Galería Manos (no. 411)*, Cuba's arts and crafts designers exhibit their original creations. Next door, a small arts and crafts market welcomes visitors to stroll around. Step by step you will be engulfed by the sounds of competing bars; from the tropical-plant patio of the *Florida* Hotel (see p. 42) and the *Café Paris (corner of San Ignacio | tel. 78 62 04 66 | Moderate)*. Step into the *Museo Farmacéutico Taqechel* in no. 155 with the sounds of a sensual bolero in the background and you will feel like the clock has been turned back a hundred years. Enjoy a drink (and WiFi hotspot) in the lobby of the *Hotel Ambos Mundos (52 rooms | corner of Mercaderes | tel. 78 60 95 30 | www.hotelambosmundos-cuba.com | Moderate–Expensive)* and take a peak in room no. 511 (*admission for non-hotel guests 2 CUC*) where Ernest Hemingway once stayed in the 1930s. His famous quote "My Mojito in La Bodeguita del Medio. My Daiquiri in El Floridita" originates from this period.

MUSEO NACIONAL DE BELLAS ARTES
(U E2) (*ṃ e2*)
The national museum of the fine arts is housed in two separate buildings: gems of Cuban painting from different centuries can be found in the modern building on Calle Trocadero *(betw. Zulueta/ Montserrate)*, while the collection of international art is housed in the former *Centro Asturiano (C/ San Rafael | betw. Zulueta/Montserrate)*, which was built in 1928 taking the Paris Opera as its model. *Both Tue–Sat 10am–5pm, Sun 10am– 2pm | combined ticket 8, individually 5 CUC each | www.museonacional.cult.cu*

MUSEO DE LA REVOLUCIÓN ●
(U E2) (*ṃ e2*)
Housed in the former Presidential Palace from 1920, the museum attracts more visitors than ever before. Crowds of tourists (mainly U.S. Americans) queue up from the entrance right down to the old city wall relics. The main attraction is *chefe en comandante* Fidel Castro (died in 2016) to whom visitors pay homage in the entrance hall; his compatriots Che Guevara and Camilo Cienfuegos are exhibited as life-size wax figures in Guerrilla uniform further upstairs, from where the tour starts and descends in chronological order. The museum gardens hold the *Memorial Granma (access via the museum)*, a huge display case with the eponymous yacht used by the 1956 rebels to land on Cuba. *Refugio 1 | betw. Monserrate/Zulueta | daily 9.30am–4pm | admission 8 CUC, guided tour additional 2 CUC*

PARQUE CENTRAL/PRADO
(U E2–3) (*ṃ e2–3*)
It is not surprising that Karl Lagerfeld specifically chose the *Paseo de Martí,* in short Prado, as a catwalk to showcase his Chanel collection in 2016. Guarded by bronze lion sculptures and lit up romantically at night by the antique bronze lanterns, this boulevard resembles a red carpet for Havana's VIPs. This shopping promenade flows into the *Parque Central* which stretches over several blocks. The open-top, hop-on hop-off buses *(10 CUC a day, diverse bus stops)* stop here and highly polished old-timers *(50 CUC for one hour)* as well as horse-drawn carriages *(1 hour round trip for 4 persons 40 CUC)* eagerly wait for passengers coming out of the surrounding luxury hotels. These include the *Parque Central Hotel* (see p. 42), behind which towers the *Edificio Bacardí* – the city's most splendid art déco building – or from the *Kempinski Grand Hotel Manzana (www.kempinski.com | Expensive)* in the dazzling white *Edificio Manzana de Gomez Mena* (built in 1917). The boulevard café in the nostalgic *In-*

glaterra Hotel (83 rooms | tel. 78 60 85 93 | 78 60 85 97 | www.grancaribe.com | *Moderate*) is the perfect place to watch the busy comings and goings in the park. It's also worth an extra visit to the building next door: the restored *Gran Teatro de La Habana Alicia Alonso* where Enrico Caruso once sang. The park is dominat-

front of the former *Palacio de los Capitanes Generales (Tue–Sun 9.30am–5pm | admission 3 CUC),* the city's oldest square is a tranquil haven provided you don't come when there is a concert. A statue of Columbus, the discoverer of Cuba, stands on the patio of the former HQ of Cuba's colonial Spanish governors (1791); the in-

Havana's old city – squares, fountains and historic facades everywhere you look

ed by the grandiose *Capitol,* a 1:1 replica of the White House in Washington built in 1929. The Cuban Parliament has plans to relocate here in 2018. When they do so, the politicians will have spiritual guidance close at hand: the *Museo de los Orishas (daily 9am–4.30pm | admission 5 CUC)* located on Paseo del Prado no. 615 gives an insight into the Afro-Cuban Gods. The Barrio Chino also stands as a shadow of the past. Thousands of Chinese, who were lured here to work under false pretences after slavery had been abolished in Cuba, once lived here. The remaining few who have stayed give the Calle Cuchillo its Asian flair.

PLAZA DE ARMAS (U F2) (*Ω f2*)

Lined with shade trees, benches and the sound-absorbing wooden brick road in

side is dedicated to the city's history. On the opposite side of the square stands the equally grandiose *Hotel Santa Isabel (27 rooms | tel. 78 60 82 01 | hotelsantaisabel. com | Expensive)* which is housed in the Palacio de los Condes de Santovenia, the former residence of the counts of Santovenia. On the left, the *El Templete* (1828) chapel is inconspicuous in comparison. In fact, the chapel was erected at the historic point where Havana's first Mass was held for the La Villa San Cristóbal de La Habana in 1519. The imposing and indomitable *Castillo de la Real Fuerza* (1577) next door was the city's first point of defence and is today Havana's oldest fortification. Do you see the tiny figure which crowns the fortress? That is *Giraldilla*, Havana's landmark. It is believed to be Inés de Bobadilla who is keeping lookout for her husband, the Cuban governor Hernando de Soto, little knowing that he had sadly died of fever at the Mississippi River. The original of Havana's oldest cast (1630) can be seen at the entrance of the INSIDERTIP ▶ *Museo de Navegación (Tue–Sun 9.30am–5pm | admission 3 CUC).* Inside, the museum houses a large scale model of a galleon, a reminder of Havana's illustrious past as the first royal shipyard in Spain's New Colonies.

PLAZA DE LA CATEDRAL (U F2) (*Ш f2*)

Habana vieja's "courtyard": tourist meeting place, open air stage, photo backdrop. The square is dominated by the baroque shell-limestone façade of the *San Cristóbal cathedral.* Begun in 1748 by the Jesuits, it housed Columbus' remains until 1898. Opposite the cathedral, the former *Palace of the Count of Bayona* (1720) shelters the *Museo de Arte Colonial (Tue–Sun 9.30am–5pm | admission 3 CUC),* which shows precious exhibits from the colonial period. Adorned with pretty arcades, the building housing the trendy *El Patio* restaurant *(tel. 78 67 10 35 | daily noon–midnight | Moderate)* used to be the palace of the Counts of Aguas Claras; the restaurant serves good Creole food. Art lovers will be interested in the *Centro de Arte Contemporáneo Wifredo Lam (C/ San Ignacio 22/corner of Empedrado | Mon–Sat 10am–5pm | admission 3 CUC)* on the left-hand side of the cathedral, which hosts the biennial of Havana *(www.bienalhabana.cult.cu; next date: 2020.).* The arts centre is named after the Cuban artist Wifredo Lam (1902–82), who studied art in Madrid, was in contact with the Surrealists in Paris and also lived in New York for a while.

PLAZA VIEJA (U F3) (*Ш f3*)

The square that never sleeps ever since it served as the most important market and trading square in the middle of the 16th century. The most imposing house, adorned with a cast-iron balcony, is the *Casa del Conde de Jaruco* (1768). The *Gómez Vila* (1909) at the corner houses the *Cámara oscura (daily 9am–6pm | admission 2 CUC),* which gives an overview of the surroundings in real-time projection. At the *Taberna La Muralla (daily | corner of C/ La Muralla | Budget–Moderate),* good food awaits as well as at the *Café el Escorial (daily 9am–9pm | Budget–Moderate)* in the evenings. In the Calle Oficios 254/ Muralla close by (towards the port), Cuba's "second explorer" is honoured at the *Casa Alejandro Humboldt (Tue–Sun 9am–5pm | admission free):* Alexander von Humboldt explored Cuba between 1800 and 1801.

CITY WALL/MUSEO CASA NATAL DE JOSÉ MARTÍ (U F4) (*Ш f4*)

Train station districts often have a shady reputation, none more so than Havana's main station district around the Calle Paula. Cuba's freedom fighter and poet José Martí grew up here. His birth place, the *Casa Natal de José Martí (C/ Leonor Pérez 314 | Tue–Sat 9am–5pm | admission 2 CUC),* stands across from the train station, currently closed due to reconstruction. In between are the remains of the old city fortifications.

FOOD & DRINK

INSIDERTIP ▶ 304 O'REILLY (U E–F2) (*Ш e–f2*)

Trendy spot for fans of tacos and fresh (sea)food such as ceviche. Excellent cocktails. *Daily noon –midnight | O'Reilly 304/ betw. Habana/Aguiar | tel. 0 52 64 47 25 | Budget–Moderate*

CAFÉ DEL ANGEL – JACQUELINE FUMERO (U E2) (*Ш e2*)

Good place to leave Havana's nostalgic past behind you. The stylish boulevard restaurant owned by the Cuban fashion designer Jaqueline Fumero is particularly popular among young people. The café also serves INSIDER TIP good breakfasts. *Daily 7.30am–10.30pm | Compostela 1/corner of Cuarteles | tel. 78 01 51 62 | Budget*

CASTILLO DE FARNÉS (U E2) (*ω e2*)
The waiter will be happy to show you the table where Fidel Castro, his brother Raúl, and Che Guevara sat on 9 January 1959. A photograph documents the event. The food is good and good-value too. *Daily noon–midnight | Av. Monserrate 401/corner Obrapía | tel. 78 67 10 30 | Moderate*

CASTROPOL (U D–E2) (*ω d–e2*)
The location of this chic restaurant on the Malecón is reason enough to eat here. Also run by the Sociedad Asturiana like the *Los Nardos (Paseo del Prado 563 | Moderate–Expensive)*. *Daily noon–midnight | Malecón 107 | tel. 78 61 48 64 | Budget–Moderate*

LA GUARIDA (UC2) (*ω c2*)
Since parts of the 1994 film "Fresa y chocolate" were filmed here, this *paladar* is often fully booked, so reserve a table! *Daily noon–4pm, 7pm–midnight | C/ Concordia 418 | betw. Gervasio/Escobar | 3rd floor | tel. 78 66 90 47 | www.laguerida. com | Expensive*

INSIDER TIP IVAN CHEFS JUSTO (U E2) (*ω e2*)
Private restaurant run by star chef Ivan. His oyster cocktail or calabash cream starters are to die for. *Daily noon–midnight | Aguacate 9 | corner of Chacón | tel. 78 63 96 97 | mobile tel. 0 53 43 85 40 | Moderate–Expensive*

SAN CRISTÓBAL (U C–D3) (*ω c–d3*)
Walls adorned with original photos of pre-revolutionary (show) stars, furnished with second-hand deco: excellent cuisine served in a delightful atmosphere. Chef's recommendation: filet of steak in a pepper sauce. *Mon–Sat noon–midnight | San Rafael 469 | tel. 78 67 91 09 | Moderate*

LA VITROLA (U F3) (*ω f3*)
Be patient: you just have to wait until a table becomes free. This authentic, privately owned corner pub on the Plaza Vieja not only serves excellent cocktails but also inexpensive, hearty food such as chicken cordon bleu. *Daily 8am–midnight | C/ San Ignacio/corner of Muralla (Plaza Vieja) | tel. 0 52 85 71 11 | www. lavitrolacuba.com | Budget–Moderate*

SHOPPING

CALLE AGUÍAR ("SCISSORS STREET") (U E2) (*ω e2*)
A huge pair of scissors in front of the tiny pedestrianised zone points the way to Havana's most famous hairdressers. On the upper floor of Calle Aguíar no. 10, Gilberto Valladares, aka "Papito", runs a mixture of a hair salon and museum called *Arte Corte (Mon–Sat noon–6pm)*. Every item in this novel salon has a story to tell, even the chair on which clients sit for their haircut. Take a stroll past the restaurants and on the left-hand side you'll see the basement boutique *Pedro's (no. 17)* which specialises in elegant casual clothing. *Between C/ Peña Pobre and C/ Santelmo*

INSIDER TIP MEMORIES (U D2) (*ω d2*)
Vintage Cuban posters, postcards, books, newspapers, curiosities and other memorabilia: This tiny store is a paradise for nostalgic Cuba fans. *Animas 57/betw. Prado/Zulueta | www.tiendamemories.com*

MUSEO DEL CHOCOLATE (U F3) (*ω f3*)
With a bit of luck you can watch them prepare the mouth-watering pralines

before buying them. Or try a glass of delicious drinking chocolate from Baracoa! *C/ Mercaderes 255 | corner Amargura*

REAL FÁBRICA DE TABACOS PARTAGÁS
● (U E3) (*ᗰ e3*)
Reputed to be the only factory in Cuba that is still producing cigars since it was founded in 1845 – it has however relocated from its historical building in C/ Industria 524 to the nearby *Calle San Carlos* 816 a few years ago. Tickets to visit the factory are available from hotels. The cigars can now be bought in the original factory building.

ENTERTAINMENT

LA BODEGUITA DEL MEDIO ●
(U F2) (*ᗰ f2*)
Home of the *Mojito*. Its walls are covered in photos of fans, the most famous being Hemingway; however it was the English admiral Sir Francis Drake who is said to have introduced the cocktail to Cuba in the 16th century. *C/ Empedrado 207 | tel. 78 67 13 74 | daily noon–0:45am*

CHACÓN 162 (U E2) (*ᗰ e2*)
Featuring a Harley-Davidson above the bar, motorcycling motifs and Route 66 signs, this authentic corner-spot pub is dedicated to bikers; you can also pay in euros or U.S. dollars (as well as CUC and CUP). *Daily 10.30am–midnight | Chacón 162/corner Callejón de Espada | tel. 78 60 13 86*

HABANA 61 (U E2) (*ᗰ e2*)
Cool Miami-style restaurant bar: Black painted, neon light walls, white bucket seats on the marble floor, serving light Cuban classics with a fresh twist. *Daily noon–2pm | C/ Habana 61 | tel. 78 01 64 33 | www.paladarhabana61.com*

INSIDER TIP SIA KAVA CAFÉ
(U D3) (*ᗰ d3*)
Could be that this insider cocktail bar will soon be chock-a-block with members of the Cuban parliament as it sits just behind the Capitol. Authentically decorated and features a snug corner hidden behind a curtain of ties. *Daily noon–2am | C/ Barcelona 502/C/ Industria*

All for show: barkeeper mixing mojitos at the Bodeguita del Medio

WHERE TO STAY

CASA AMISTAD (U D3) (*ᗰ d3*)
Light and nicely furnished flat in an old building, home to German documentary filmmaker Jochen Beckmann. Central and quiet location on 2nd floor with roof terrace; Betty and Ciro look after guests, also self-catering. *4 rooms | C/ Amistad 378 | corner Barcelona | tel. 78 60 14 32 | www.casa-amistad.net | Budget*

CASA COLONIAL CARY Y NILO (U C2) (*📖 c2*)

Everyone feels at home at Cary's and Nilo's, an elderly couple who witnessed the revolution first hand when they were young. *3 air-conditioned en-suite rooms | C/ Gervasio 216 | betw. Concor-*

PARQUE CENTRAL (U E3) (*📖 e3*)

There's a fair bit of luxury hiding behind the remaining façade of a 17th-century palace; the house has a central location. In the lobby, even non-residents can use WiFi (8 CUC/hr.). *279 rooms | C/ Neptuno | betw. Paseo del Prado/Zulueta | tel.*

Restored to its former colonial glory: the Hotel Sevilla

dia/Virtudes | tel. 78 62 71 09 | orixl@ yahoo.es | Budget

FLORIDA (U F2) (*📖 f2*)

On the pretty patio you'll feel like you've travelled back in time. From 10pm onwards, the smoky **INSIDERTIP** *Magato* piano bar *(admission 10 CUC)* becomes a spot for good salsa dancers. *25 rooms | C/ Obispo 252/corner Cuba | tel. 78 62 41 27 | www.gaviotahotels.com | Expensive*

LOS FRAILES (U F3) (*📖 f3*)

Altar images, religious art and staff dressed in monk's cowls create a contemplative atmosphere in this former palace. *22 rooms | C/ Teniente Rey 8 | betw. Oficios/Mercaderes | tel. 78 62 93 83 | www. gaviotahotels.com | Moderate–Expensive*

78 60 66 27 | www.hotelparquecentral. com | Expensive

RAQUEL (U F3) (*📖 f3*)

Grandiose art nouveau hotel, famous for its stained-glass dome and the good views from the ● ☼ roof terrace, one of the most beautiful chill-out spaces in the entire Old Town. Spacious rooms. *25 rooms | C/ Amargura 103 | corner San Ignacio | www.hotelraquel.com | Moderate*

SEVILLA (U E2) (*📖 e2*)

A gem from the early 20th century; the elegant ☼ rooftop garden yields fine views of the Old Town. *181 rooms | C/ Trocadero 55 | betw. Paseo de Marti/Zulueta | tel. 78 60 85 60 | www.hotelsevillacuba.com | Expensive*

HOSTAL VALENCIA (U F3) *(📖 f3)*
This friendly little guesthouse with its cosy courtyard has only 12 rooms, all however equipped with air-conditioning and bathroom. *C/ Oficios 53/Obrapía | tel. 78 67 10 37 | hostal-valencia.hava nacityhotels.com | Moderate*

INFORMATION

INFOTUR (U E2) *(📖 e2)*
Obispo 524 | betw. Bernaza/Villegas | tel. 78 66 33 33; Obispo/San Ignacio | tel. 78 63 68 84 | www.infotur.cu

EXCURSIONS

AVENTOURA (U E2) *(📖 e2)*
With branches all over Cuba, the Havana office of this travel agency offers excursions to Cayo Levisa, Vinales, Varadero or Trinidad. *Mon–Sat 10am–6pm | Monserrate 261 | Edificio Bacardí | tel. 78 63 28 00 | www.aventoura.de*

MIRAMAR/ VEDADO

(U A1–3) *(📖 a1–3)* **Vedado was once no-man's land, state territory and a district nobody dared to enter (vedado means "forbidden").**
The rich invaded the quarter at the start of the 20th century and built their villas here while US aristocracy opened up hotels, casinos and bars. Main streets such as La Rampa, Línea and Calzada and broad boulevards such as the Avenida de los Presidentes and Paseo were laid out. The latter leads to the Plaza de la Revolución. On Calle L, on a hill, you'll find the main entrance to the University of Havana, "La Colina" for short. Stone blocks with street numbers at the junc-

tions help with orientation. During the prohibition era in the US, when the centre of Vedado turned into a sin strip of bars, the wealthy moved further west, to *Miramar*. This quarter begins where the Malecón ends. Its main artery is the most glorious street in the Caribbean, ★ *Avenida Quinta.* It leads into the world of the top embassies and company headquarters, as well as the aristocratic homes of noble families, new luxury hotels, and to Marina Hemingway.

SIGHTSEEING

CEMENTERIO COLÓN
The grave of Rinti, the dog who did not leave her mistress' side even when she died is truly moving. A stroll around the cemetery offers an insight into Cuban

LOW BUDGET

A comfortable and cheap way to get around Havana's Old Town are the *bici-taxis* (bike rickshaws). A trip will only set you back around 2–3 CUC.

Sightseeing as much as you like for 5 CUC a day: hop-on-hop-off buses ply three routes that may be combined: Old Town, Playas del Este (departure across from Hotel *Inglaterra*), Miramar (departure from Plaza de la Revolución/same stop as Old Town bus).

● A carriage ride through the Old Town doesn't have to be expensive if you share the fun and price *(40 CUC/hr., 4 pers.)* with friends or other tourists. Lean back and enjoy the two-horsepower trip (from Parque Central).

history with stories of the many writers, politicians and revolutionaries buried here. These include writer Alejo Carpentier (1904–80) and the Buena Vista Social Club star Ibrahim Ferrer (1927–2005). The oldest part of the cemetery, used until 1875, is the subterranean *Galería de Tobías*, which was inaugurated by the architect of the cemetery, Calixto de Loira, a year after it was founded. *Av. Obispo Fray Jacinto and C/ 14 | Entrance: Zapata and C/ 12 | daily 8am–5pm | admission 5 CUC*

1920s for María Gómez Mena, Countess of Revilia de Camargo, the villa shelters precious exhibits, including Sèvres porcelain, Chippendale furniture and exquisite silver work. The palace was framed by a well-planned garden: to the right, flowers blossomed according to the different seasons, to the left the "night" garden brought coolness. *C/ 17, no. 502 | betw. D and E | Tue–Sat 10.30am–6pm | admission 3 CUC*

A dramatical staging of death: headstones on the Cementerio Colón

MUSEO COMPAY SEGUNDO

In the house where Compay Segundo (1907–2003) lived, photographs and documents tell of the life of the Buena Vista Social Club star musician. *Miramar | C/ 22, no. 103 | corner 1ra/3ra | Mon–Fri 9.30am–3pm | free admission | tel. 72 06 86 29 | www.compay-segundo.com*

MUSEO NACIONAL DE ARTES DECORATIVAS

Cuba's most opulent example of noble living in pre-revolutionary times: built in the

PARQUE JOHN LENNON

The place to go for Beatles fans. A bronze statue of the iconic John Lennon sits on a park bench waiting for you to join him. A security guard is employed to guard Lennon's glasses (after they were repeatedly stolen) and if you offer him a tip he will let you put them on for a selfie. Built by José Villa Soberón, the life-size statue was unveiled on the 20th anniversary of the ex-Beatle's death by none other than Fidel Castro, apparently himself an admirer of Lennon. By the way John Lennon never actually visited Cuba. *Vedado | between Calles 17 and 15, 6 and 8*

PLAZA DE LA REVOLUCIÓN
(U A5) (𝄞 a5)

Havana's population bid their last farewell to Fidel Castro on this square at the end of 2016. Workers traditionally gather here on May 1 to celebrate Labour Day. The square is the heart of the revolution! The "Catalan Hill" has been dominated by the 109 m (358 ft) high *Memorial a José Martí (Mon–Sat 9.30am–4.30pm | admission 5 CUC)* since 1958. Many representative buildings are located around the plaza: the *Teatro Nacional* (corner Paseo), the Ministries of the Interior (with Guevara on the facade), the information centre (with Cienfuegos on the facade), the National Library, the Ministry of the Defence, the *Palacio de la Revolución* and the seat of the PCC Communist Party.

FOOD & DRINK

EL ALJIBE

Does succulently marinated chicken sound tasty to you? Then head to this cult restaurant in Miramar to enjoy all different types of *pollo* (chicken). You will not regret it. *Daily noon–midnight | Av. 7a | betw. Calle 24 and 26 | tel. 72 04 15 83 | Budget–Moderate*

INSIDER TIP ▶ ATELIER

Dine elegantly in between modern artworks. The food is also creative, as evidenced by e.g. salmon rolls with cheese or *malangitas* with a honey dip (malanga is a kind of Caribbean cabbage, finely grated, mixed with egg and deep-fried). *Daily noon–midnight | C/ 5ta no. 511 | betw. Paseo and C/ 2 | tel. 78 36 20 25 | Moderate*

HELADERÍA COPPELIA (U A2) (𝄞 a2)

Famous through the "Fresa y Chocolate" film, this ice-cream palace of 1966 continues to be a popular meeting place on the La Rampa/Calle L. crossroads in Vedado. *Tue–Sun 11am–10pm*

EL IDILIO

Alone the smells of sizzling langoustines, fish filets and meat from the barbecue are enough to whet your appetite at this outdoor paladar. *Daily noon–midnight | C/ G 351 | corner C/ 15 | tel. 78 30 79 21 | www.idiliocuba.com | Budget–Moderate*

PP'S TEPPANYAKI (U A2) (𝄞 a2)

The privately run Japanese restaurant situated on the first floor of an apartment building has a large following of fans. *Daily 6pm–11pm | C/ 21, no. 104 | betw. C/ L and M (next to La Roca) | tel. 78 36 25 30 | Moderate– Expensive*

EL TOCORORO

This restaurant was once the "prima donna" among Havana' restaurants – the photos on the wall with special guests such as Gabriel García Márquez provide the evidence. Today the traditional style and atmosphere are accentuated by candlelight and sophisticated live music. Suitable for a special occasion. *Mon–Sat noon–midnight | C/ 18 | corner Av. 3ra | tel. 72 04 22 09 | Moderate*

SPORTS & ACTIVITIES

MARINA HEMINGWAY

Cuba's largest marina is equipped with everything the sailor needs: restaurants, shops, hotels. Diving and snorkelling trips can be arranged here. *5ta Av. 248 | tel. 72 04 50 88 | www.nauticamarlin. com*

ENTERTAINMENT

CABARET TROPICANA ★

World-famous dance revue in glitzy costumes where the best revue girls in Cuba

Opulent glamour show for tourists: Cabaret Tropicana

take to the stage. This revue theatre was founded in 1939 by Cuban artist Victor de Correa. *C/ 72 | betw. 41 and 45 | tel. 72 67 17 17 | daily from 8pm, show from 10pm | admission depending on cover 75, 85 or 95 CUC | www.cabaret-tropicana.com*

CAFÉ CANTANTE (U A4) (𝄞 a4)

The best live salsa bands take the dance floor to boiling point. The entrance to the cellar bar is to the side of the Teatro Nacional. *Av Paseo/Plaza de la Revolución | tel. 78 78 42 73 | daily 8pm–3am | admission from 5–15 CUC*

CAFÉ JAZZ MIRAMAR

Fresh, clean air and great acoustics at this non-smoking jazz & blues club where Cuba's jazz masters regularly play together. *5ta Av. 9401/betw. C/ 94 and 96 (Cine Teatro Miramar) | tel. 0 53 20 09 33 | Tue–Sun from 10.30pm | admission 5 CUC*

CASA DE LA MÚSICA

Concerts in the house of the Egrem music studios; the attached shop is a must for aficionados of Cuban music. *C/ 20/corner C/ 35 | tel. 72 04 04 47 | daily 10pm–3am | admission 10–20 CUC*

DON CANGREJO

By day a fairly modest fish restaurant, in the evenings a boheme meeting point with super ambience under the stars, with pool and right by the sea. *Av. 1ra | betw. 16 and 18 | tel. 72 04 50 02*

FÁBRICA DE ARTE

This cultural centre owned by rock star X Alfonso attracts Cuba's avant garde with art and events. Next door is the trendy rooftop club **INSIDER TIP** *El Cocinero*. *Thu–Sat 8pm–4am, Sun 8pm–2am | C/ 26/ corner C/ 11 | Vedado*

LA TORRE ⚓ (U A2) (𝄞 a2)

Havana at your feet: The bar crowns the top of the towering *Edificio FOCSA* (the city's highest building with 36 floors). Only take a seat at the tables next to the ceiling-to-floor windows if you have a head for heights. *C/ 17, between C/ M and N | tel. 78 38 30 88 | daily noon–midnight*

WHERE TO STAY

LA CASA DE MARY

If you're traveling by car, this pleasant house offers tranquil accommodation in this quiet villa district. The city is in easy reach along La Rampa. Lovely hosts. *1 en-suite room, air conditioned | C/ 21, no. 1417/corner C/ 28 | Vedado | tel. 78 30 19 33 | Budget*

HABANA RIVIERA ∿ (U A1) (*ਯ a1*)

Built by U.S. mafia boss Meyer Lansky and unveiled by Ginger Rogers in 1957, this magnificent Fifties-style hotel has an illustrious history – and the famous salsa bar *Copa Room. 352 rooms | Av. Malecón/corner Paseo | Vedado | tel. 78 33 40 51 | www.hotelhavanariviera.com | Moderate–Expensive*

MELIÁ/TRYP HOTELS

The *Meliá Cohiba (462 rooms | C/ Paseo | betw. C/ 1a/C/ 3a | tel. 7 33 36 36)* with its chic **INSIDER TIP** *Habana Café (8pm–2.30am | daily dance show 10 CUC)* is the number one place to be in Vedado. The former Hilton which was rechristened *Habana Libre* after the revolution and became its headquarters, also belongs to Meliá group as Tryp Habana Libre (*572 rooms | C/ L/corner C/ 23 | Vedado | tel. 78 34 61 00, 7 33 38 04*); at the *Torquino club (daily 10.30pm–3am)* on the 25th floor, **INSIDER TIP** the roof opens up at midnight (dress elegantly); for all: *www.meliacuba.com | Expensive*

NACIONAL DE CUBA ★ (U B2) (*ਯ b2*)

Cast-iron elevator grilles, luxurious dining rooms and salons: built in 1930 with mafia monies, this top-notch establishment welcomed Hollywood stars such as Errol Flynn, Marlon Brando and Ava Gardner – before the revolution, of course. The *Cabaret Parisien* puts on a top revue show. *427 rooms | C/ O/corner 21 | Vedado | tel. 78 36 35 64 | www.hotelnacionaldecuba.com | Expensive*

ORESTES Y MAGALY (U B2) (*ਯ b2*)

Stay in the former U.S. amusement district, with balconies overlooking the Hotel *Nacional* and the sea. Just steps away from the cabaret bar *Salon Rojo,* La Rampa (the street lined with agents), Hotel *Libre* and the ice palace *Coppelia*: both rooms (each with separate bathroom) are in a 7th floor apartment of the Edificio Altamira. *C/ O no. 58, betw. C/ 19 and 21 | tel. 78 32 97 80 | Budget*

EXCURSIONS

CARIBBEAN TOURS (U E2) (*ਯ e2*)

The Swiss Cuba expert runs an office in Vedado. The *Customer Experience* department helps you with the booking of excursions. *Av. Paseo 606 | betw. C/ 25 and 27 | tel. 7 8 34 42 51 | www.caribbeantours.ch*

INFORMATION

INFOTUR

The state-owned tourist information centre has its office in the Playa district of Miramar. *Mon–Sat 9am–5pm, Sun 9am–noon | 5ta Av./C/ 112 | tel. 72 04 70 36 | www.infotur.cu*

HAVANA'S EAST AND SOUTH

Built in 1958, the tunnel in Havana connects the port to its bay and transports you quickly to the attractions in the east of the city.

It merges into the four-lane Vía Monumental which forms a crossroads with the Vía Blanca shortly after the exit to the fishing village of Cojímar. This road takes you in one direction to *Playas del Este,* the popular beaches visited by city dwellers, and in the opposite, to Guanabacoa, Havana's Afro-Cuban quarter. Whoever wants to head from Cojímar to the Hemingway museum of San Francisco de Paula should return along the *Vía Monumental* (will soon be called *1er Anillo de la Habana)* and continue for a further 15 km/9 miles to the exit at San Francisco de Paula (or Calzada de Guines). If you carry on without stopping, you'll reach the deep south of Havana, at the golf club, airport or the recreation area of *Parque Lenín* (see p. 109) – and can return to the centre along the Avenida Independencia.

SIGHTSEEING

COJÍMAR (130 A2) (*ﬂ D2*)
Pretty fishing resort where Hemingway anchored his boat "Pilar", made friendships with fishermen, notably Gregorio Fuentes (1897–2002), and was inspired to write his book "The Old Man and the Sea". Today you can enjoy its relaxed suburban setting, hang out at Hemingway's favourite bar *La Terraza (daily 11am–11pm | C/ Mart Real 161 | tel. 7 93 92 32 | Moderate–Expensive)* and visit the Hemingway monument on Malecón and the small fortress *El Torreón* (1649).

MUSEO HEMINGWAY ★ ●
Hemingway's house lies in San Francisco de Paula, on the edge of Havana, approx. a 20 minutes' drive south of the Old Town. Furniture, hunting trophies, countless books, photos, documents and private mementoes – all has been left the way Ernest Hemingway (1899–1961) himself once left it. The writer purchased the Finca La Vigía in 1940. In the garden you can see the swimming pool in which Ava Gardner swam naked, the dog cemetery and the yacht "Pilar". *Finca La Vigía | Mon–Sat 10am–4.30pm | admission 5 CUC | www.hemingwaycuba.com*

MUSEO HISTÓRICO DE GUANABACOA ●
This museum is dedicated to the various Santería deities, exhibiting ornate costumes, scary fetishes, cult artefacts and amazing photos of various ceremonies. What may be unsettling to visitors is a faith accepted as part of everyday life by most Cubans. *C/ Marti 108 | betw. San Antonio/Versalles | Tue–Sat 10am–6pm, Sun 10am–1pm | admission 2, guided tour 1, photo permit 5, video 25 CUC*

PLAYAS DEL ESTE ★
(130 A–B2) (*ﬂ E2*)
The favourite weekend retreat of Havanan locals: 60 km/37 miles of beaches in Havana's east. The first of these, the narrow *Playa Bacuranao*, is reached in 20 minutes from Malecón through the tunnel and along the Vía Blanca. The widest, the *Playa Santa María,* has developed into a small yet popular tourist centre. Hotel tip: *Aparthotel Islazul Las Terrazas (62 ap. with TV | Av. de Las Terrazas | betw. C/ 10/Rotonda | tel. 7 97 13 44 | www.islazul.cu | Budget–Moderate).* The last post along the Playas del Este is the *Playa Jibacoa* at km 60 on the Vía Blanca with the *Memories Jibacoa (250 rooms | www.memoriesresorts.com | Expensive),* an all-inclusive resort with three speciality restaurants, spa and diving centre. This beach is situated in the new province of Mayabeque (founded in 2011). Head 20 km/12.5 miles further along the Vía Blanca to its highlight, the 112 m/367 ft high *Puente Bacunayagua* bridge suspended above the breathtaking Valle Yumurí far below.

A SHORT HOP BY PLANE FROM HAVANA

ISLA DE LA JUVENTUD
(129 D–E 5–6) (*ᗪ C–D 3–4*)

Shipwrecks, pirate legends and a treasure found here nurture the legend that the island once called Isla de Pinos (Pine Island) is Stevenson's "Treasure Island". For Castro it was his prison island. Today, the *Presidio Modelo (on the Nueva Gerona–Playa Bibijagua road | Mon–Sat 8am–4pm, Sun 8am–noon | admission 2 CUC)*, a mass prison where Fidel did time in 1953–55 after the failed storming of the Moncada Barracks, is a museum. Later, Castro renamed the island *Isla de la Juventud* (Youth Island), turning it into a centre of youth exchange.

Nueva Gerona (pop. 85,000) has a ferry port, eateries, amongst them the popular Paladar *El Caney (daily | C/ 3ra 401 | betw. C/ 4 and 6 | Budget)*, a number of *casas particulares* and the hotels *Rancho del Tesoro (35 rooms | Ctra. La Fe, km 2.5 | tel. 46 32 30 35, Budget)* and *Villa Isla de la Juventud (currently closed)*. Two museums: the *Museo Finca El Abra (Ctra. de Siguanea, km 2.5 | Tue–Sat 9am–4pm, Sun 9am–noon)* on the edge of town, where José Martí recuperated from his prison term in Havana in 1870, and the *Museo Municipal (Parque Central | Tue–Sat 9am–6pm, Sun 9am–1pm | both 1 CUC admission)*. If you want to go for a dip, you'll find the black sand of *Playa Bibijagua* to the east.

The most beautiful beach lies 60 km (37 miles) outside the town in a nature reserve on the southern coast that can only be visited with a guide or authorisation. There are caves with pre-Columbian rock paintings: the *Cueva de Punta del Este* and *Cueva Finlay*. Trips can be arranged through *Ecotur (C/ 24/esq. C/47 | tel. 46 32 71 01 | ecoturij@enet.cu)*. Divers will find their needs met at the *El Colony hotel (77 rooms | Ctra. Siguanea, km 42 | tel. 46 39 81 81 | www.hotelelcolony.com | Budget)*. The 56 diving spots are scattered around the Punta Francés. *www.isladelajuventud-cuba.com*

A miniature-like fortress: El Torreón in Cojímar

THE WEST

Elusively old mountains and red-soil tobacco fields, Caribbean's largest swamp and the island's most picturesque beach: Cuba's westerly region is home to many surprising contrasts.

The nearest to the capital of Havana is the Sierra del Rosario, up to 800m/2600 ft high. It is home to many rare species of plants and animals that only occur on Cuba, and was declared a Unesco biosphere reserve in 1985. Back in the 19th century, Americans were already taking (spa) holidays in San Diego de los Baños, where the Sierra del Rosario turns into the Sierra de los Órganos, long before the 1920s, when they chose Varadero as their new favourite spot.

The mountain ranges mark the beginning of the tobacco province of Pinar del Río with the eponymous capital. Here, the best soils and most famous *vegas* (tobacco cultivation areas) of the world of cigars join the greatest scenic attraction in Cuba, the limestone mountains called *mogotes* in the Valle de Viñales, as well as another Unesco biosphere reserve, the Guanahacabibes National Park on the peninsula of the same name, Cuba's westernmost point.

No less exciting destinations await east of Havana. The Vía Blanca takes you to Cuba's most famous resort: Varadero. And the Autopista Central shows the way to the Caribbean's largest swamp area, the Ciénaga de Zapata, where crocodiles and in the coastal waters the rare manatees find respite from human intervention.

Look forward to forests, imposing limestone mountains, tobacco fields, jungle-like swamps and the famous beach of Varadero

PINAR DEL RÍO

(128 C4) *(∭ C3)* **Situated at the heart of Cuba's most fertile region, the affluent provincial capital of Pinar del Río (150,000 inhabitants) is Cuba's undisputed capital of tobacco.**

Founded in 1669, Pinar del Río has since lived well off the nicotine plant. Today, the town also manufactures solar panels for international export. Tourism plays less of a role – yet what the town lacks in the way of sightseeing attractions, it compensates with its metropolitan flair.

SIGHTSEEING

FÁBRICA DE GUAYABITA

Using time-honoured recipes, a delicious liqueur is produced here from the guava fruit and sold. *C/ Isabel Rubio 189 | tel. 48 75 29 66 | Mon–Fri 9am–4pm | guided tour 1 CUC*

Laboriously picked by hand: tobacco grower harvesting leaves at Pinar del Río

FÁBRICA DE TABACOS FRANCISCO DONATIÉN ●

Watch the *tabaqueros* at work; in the shop (also open Sat 8.30am–1pm) you can buy INSIDER TIP▶ Robaina cigars from the most famous Cuban family-run factory. *C/ Maceo 157 | Mon–Fri 9am–4pm | guided tour 5 CUC*

PALACIO GUASH (MUSEO DE CIENCIAS NATURALES)

The doctor Francisco Guash Ferrer immortalised himself by building in the curious mix of styles seen at Palacio Guash (1909). Amongst the attractions on show at the natural history museum housed here today are seashells, snails, moths and fossils, and not only children like the almost life-size figures of two dinosaurs. *C/ Martí 202 | Mon–Sat 9am–4:45pm, Sun 9am–1pm | admission 2 CUC*

FOOD & DRINK

PALADAR EL MESÓN

The private restaurant opened in 2005 as a tiny *paladar* and is still the best address for Cuban cuisine. *Mon–Sat noon–10pm | C/ Martí 205 | betw. Pinares/Pacheco | tel. 48 75 28 67 | Budget*

RESTAURANT CABARET RUMAYOR

Rustic state-run restauant. The smoked fried chicken is the speciality. Thu–Sun there's a dancing show from 10pm. *Wed–Mon noon–9.30pm | Ctra. Viñales, km 1 | tel. 48 76 30 07 | Budget–Moderate*

WHERE TO STAY

VUELTABAJO

Centrally located hotel, nicely decorated with works by local artists. The INFOTUR stall in the lobby provides information about the countryside. *39 rooms | C/ Martí 103 | corner Rafael Morales | tel. 48 75 93 81 | www.islazul.cu | Budget*

WHERE TO GO

MARÍA LA GORDA (128 B5) (*Ø B3*)

The 139 km/87 miles of road from Pinar del Río south to María La Gorda (3 hrs, some of the road is in a bad state)

are worth exploring for more reasons than one. For one thing, it starts out by passing the world's best tobacco-growing area, the *Vuelta abajo,* in the triangle between Pinar, San Juan y Martínez and San Luis. In the Cuchillas de Barbacoa of San Juan y Martínez you'll discover famous *vegas* (tobacco plantations) such as *Las Vegas de Robaina,* a family concern since 1845. In the south, the Guanahacabibes peninsula, with its biosphere reserve, arches like a high-heel boot around the Bahía de Corrientes. Located 3 km/1.9 mile away from the *Roncali* lighthouse is the comfortable Gaviota hotel INSIDER TIP *Villa Cabo San Antonio (16 bungalows | Extensión 204 | tel. 48 75 76 76, 48 75 01 18 | Moderate)* on the Playa las Tumbas. Bikes for hire. Divers and beach lovers head for the heel of the boot, to María la Gorda with its diving hotel *Villa María La Gorda (71 rooms | tel. 48 77 80 77 | www.hotelmarialagorda-cuba.com | Moderate).* Day trips by bus are offered by Transtur in Pinar del Rio.

SAN DIEGO DE LOS BAÑOS
(129 D3) (*C2*)

A good 50 km/31 miles before Pinar del Río, a road branches off from the motorway and takes you into a mountainous region rich in minerals which attracted U.S. Americans as far back as the 19th century. The most famous spring is in San Diego de los Baños. You can try the curative powers of the warm water (30–40°C) in the *Balneario* at the *Hotel Mirador (30 rooms | C/ 23 Final | tel. 48 77 83 38 | www.islazul.cu | Budget).* The hotel offers day trips into the *La Güira* national park and to the INSIDER TIP *Cueva de los Portales*, Che Guevara's headquarters during the Cuban missile crisis.

SOROA (129 D3) (*D2*)
The attraction of Soroa, halfway between Pinar and Havana in the Artemisa prov-

ince, is the magnificent *orchid garden (daily 9am–4.30pm | admission 3 CUC).* Over 700 species grow in this tropical paradise. The flowering period is between December and March. Guided tours last 30–45 minutes. The nearby *Mirador de Venus* offers glorious views. Before you get there, a path leads to the 22 m/72 ft *El Salto waterfall (daily 8am–5pm | admission 3 CUC).* Hotel: *Villa Soroa (80 rooms | Ctra. Soroa, km 8 | tel. (47) 52 35 56 | www.hotelescubanacan.com | Moderate*

LAS TERRAZAS (129 D3) (*C–D2*)
With its lake framed by picturesque mountain slopes, this eco-tourism resort in the biosphere reserve of the Sierra del Rosario near Soroa (4 km/2.5 miles) is an idyllic sight. Highlight is the *Hotel Moka (42 rooms | Autopista 4 | Candelaria–Pinar del Río, km 51 | tel. 48 77 86 00 | Moderate),* integrated into the landscape in an original way. Tickets for the park (2 CUC) and guided trips are available from the information centre *Puerto de las Delicias (tel. (47) 77 85 55 | www.lasterrazas.cu).*

⭐ **Mogotes**
Unique landscape with ancient limestone features in the Valle de Viñales → p. 54

⭐ **Mansión Xanadú**
Stay here if money is no object → p. 58

⭐ **Cayo Largo**
Island lovers will find several of them here → p. 60

⭐ **Ciénaga de Zapata**
The Caribbean's largest swamp area is a paradise for plants and animals → p. 60

MARCO POLO HIGHLIGHTS

VALLE DE VIÑALES

(128 C3) *(𝄫 B–C2)* **The scenery of this national park in the Valle de Viñales (approx. 84 sq mi, 53 km/33 miles north of Pinar del Río) lures visitors from all over the world.**

The gigantic residual limestone hills rising out of the flat red soil here are

SIGHTSEEING

CUEVA DEL INDIO

Visiting this cave is done by pleasure boat on the river that runs through the cave, Río San Vicente. If you want to spot **INSIDER TIP** thousands of bats on their collective flight out of the cave every evening, make sure to be at the exit of the cave at the *Ranchón campestre. Daily 9am–5.30pm | admission 5 CUC*

Modern art on the limestone mountain: the Mural de la Prehistoria

millions of years old. Hollowed out by subterranean streams and eroded on the outside into soft shapes, the famous ★ *mogotes* are a paradise for nature lovers, sheltering many endemic plants and birds. Travellers congregate at the small cosmopolitan town of *Viñales* (since 1607) with its many *casas particulares,* private restaurants, and the small, worthwile *Museo Municipal* (see p. 96).

MURAL DE LA PREHISTORIA

With a bit of imagination, looking at the colourful mural (1961) painted on the bare limestone wall of the *Dos Hermanos* mogote *(daily 8.30am–6pm | 3 CUC)* by Leovigildo González feels like being at the bottom of a primeval sea. The *Mural de la Prehistoria* restaurant *(daily | tel. 48 97 62 60 | Moderate)* serves pork chops with *arroz moro. Ctra. al Moncada, km 1*

FOOD & DRINK

INSIDER TIP BALCÓN DEL VALLE

A breathtaking experience: treetop restaurant with a view over the mountains. For simplicity's sake, all meals here cost 8 CUC. *Daily 8am–10pm | Ctra. a Viñales, km 23 | 120 m west of the Centro de Información | tel. 48 69 58 47 | Budget*

CASA DE DON TOMÁS

State-run restaurant in the oldest and most beautiful house in Viñales. The house cocktail "Trapiche" is delicious. *Daily 10am–10pm | C/ Salvador Cisneros 140 | tel. 48 8 93 63 00 | Moderate*

EL PALENQUE DE CIMARRONES

You reach the restaurant through a long cave corridor. What once served as a hide-out for slaves is now a popular lunch-time restaurant. *Ctra. a Puerto Esperanza, km 36 | Budget*

LEISURE & SPORTS

CENTRO DE VISITANTES

Besides providing information on the region's geography, you can also organize a guide to take you on trails *(3 hours cost from 12 CUC)* on foot or on horseback *(from 5 CUC per hour)* through the national park and to the **INSIDER TIP** *Gran Caverna de Santo Tomás*, situated just 18 km/11 miles away. With 46 km/29 miles of galleries on eight levels, it is one of the largest caves in Latin America (steep climb). *Ctra. a Pinar del Río, km 22 | tel. 48 79 61 44 | daily 8am–6pm*

ZIPLINE/CANOPY

The 1100 m/3608 ft long, up to 35 m/114 ft high zip wire experience starts at the Loma de Fortín in Moncada (5 km/3 miles from Viñales) and flies you over eight platforms and a mirador. *Daily 8am–4pm*

| 8 CUC | Ctra. a Moncada/the Viñales bus stop on the hop-on hop-off bus tour

WHERE TO STAY

HOSTAL DE GLORIA

Guests from all over the world feel at home at Señora Gloria. If her five rooms (with bath) are booked out, you can try instead her son's modern hostal *(El Bemba)*. Bikes to hire, excursions organized. *C/ Orlando Nodarse 15 | tel. 48 69 54 03 | Budget*

LOS JAZMÍNES

The number one in Viñales, meeting place for tourists from all over the world. The 🌊 pool terrace affords a fantastic view of the valley of the mogotes. *70 rooms | Ctra. de Viñales, km 25 | tel. 48 79 62 05 | Moderate*

WHERE TO GO

CAYO JUTÍAS (128 C3) (*ℳ B2*)

This tiny island with beautiful beach lies 54k km/34 miles to the northwest and can be reached via a dam. Sun huts, snorkel equipment hire, restaurant *(daily 9am–7pm | Budget). Accessible via Santa Lucía by collective taxi for approx. 20 CUC, takes 2 hrs due to very poor road conditions*

CAYO LEVISA (128–129 C–D3) (*ℳ C2*)

The island with the most beautiful beach lies approx. 50 km/31 miles to the northeast of Viñales, accessible only by ferry from Palma Rubia *(trip out daily 10am, back 5pm | 35 CUC incl. buffet lunch)*. If you'd like to stay overnight, there's the *Villa Cayo Levisa (35 rooms | tel. 48 75 65 01 | www.cubanacan.cu | Moderate)*.

GRAN CAVERNA DE SANTO TOMÁS (128 C3) (*ℳ B2*)

The ten-minute steep climb up to the cave entrance is a short test of your endurance. Be also aware that there is no artificial lighting along the 46 km/29 miles of galleries and there are some steep climbs and scrambles over slippery rocks on the 90-minute guided tour through one of the largest cave systems of its kind in Latin America. A headlamp, helmet and guide are included in the price. Make sure you wear suitable shoes. 1 km/0.6mi to the south of Moncada (signposted). *Daily 8am–4pm | admission 10 CUC | 1 km/0.6 mile south of the village El Moncada (signposted)*

VARADERO

(130 C2) (⑪ F2) **Cuba's most famous beach resort manages the vast crowds of international tourists with nonchalance – no wonder really; after the Special Period in Time of Peace (1989), Varadero was the first resort to build hotels. Its uninterrupted 20 km/12 mile beach attracted tourists even before the revolution.**

The Chilean poet Pablo Neruda described the magical beauty of its "electric coast" with its "radiant infinity of phosphorus and moon". The tiny church *Elvira* (1880) in the 1ra Avenida/Calle 47 stands as a reminder of the beginnings of this former salt mine and fishing village while the Josone park and golf site, both formerly in the possession of rich citizens, bring to mind the glory days of the past. Home to 50 hotels, many of which are 5-star resorts, and exclusive yachting harbour, Varadero (pop. 27,000) is today Cuba's main tourism hub. Located on the sinuously long Hicacos Peninsula, the resort is around 130 km/81 miles from Havana.

SIGHTSEEING

MUSEO MUNICIPAL

Among the exhibits at the pretty Carribean *Villa Abreu* (1921) are pictures of the former baseball star Fidel Castro. The Hicao tree that gave the peninsula its

On Cuba's beach peninsula of Varadero, sun & fun take centre stage

name stands in the garden. *C/ 59/corner Playa | daily 10am–7pm | admission 1 CUC*

PARQUE JOSONE

Pretty recreation park with an artificial lake, botanical rarities and restaurants on the former estate belonging to the rum baron José Fermín Iturróz from Cárdenas and his wife Onelia (the first three letters of both their names are in "Josone"). Excellent lobster served in **INSIDER TIP** *La Gruta del Vino (daily 3.30pm–10.30pm | Moderate). 1a Av. | betw. Calle 56 and 59 | daily 9am–11pm*

RESERVA ECÓLOGICA VARADERO

Varadero's green lung spreads across over 17 sq miles between hotel gardens in the east of the Hicaco peninsula. The park includes the *Cueva de Ambrosia* with cult carvings from pre-Columbian times and by escaped slaves. A *Centro Visitantes* has information on hiking trails, for example to *El Patriarca*, a 500-year-old cactus. *Autopista Sur | admission 3 CUC*

FOOD & DRINK

LA CASA DE AL

Recognisable by the gangster car. Reputedly the former villa of mafia boss Al Capone. Good, albeit expensive food. *Daily 10am–10pm | Av. Kawama/betw. hotels Villa Punta Blanca and Club Karey | tel. 45 66 80 18 | Moderate–Expensive*

KIKE-KCHO

Romantic and elegant restaurant built on stilts in the water at the Marina Gaviota; serves crawfish fresh from the seabed. *Daily noon–11pm | Autopista Sur y Final | Punta Hicacos | tel. 45 66 41 15 | Moderate–Expensive*

SALSA SUÁREZ

Paladar with small front garden, where you will be spoilt in style by the delicious, good-value dishes of the day, which could include *eperlán* (fried pargo fish balls). *Wed–Mon from noon (till the last guest leaves) | C/ 31 103 | betw. 1ra and 3ra Av. | tel. 45 52 82 10 33 | Budget*

WACO'S CLUB

Named after the Cuban Olympian Roberto Ojeda "Waco", cox of the double skull boat who came 5th in the 1992 Barcelona Olympics. This private restaurant would have taken gold for its excellent cuisine! *Daily 3.30pm–10.30pm | Av. 3ra 212 | betw. C/ 58 and 59 | tel. 45 61 21 26 | Budget–Moderate*

SHOPPING

SHOPPING CENTRES

The *Centro Comercial Hicacos (Av. 1ra | betw. C/ 44 and 46)* was established on the lower floor of the *Coppelia* ice palace. For a bigger selection, head for the *Plaza Américas (Autopista Sur, km 11)* with a few branded boutiques.

SOUVENIR MARKETS

Straw hats, T-shirts with Cuban themes, jewellery and much more is on offer from the five markets on the Avenida 1ra: *corner Calle 12, corner Calle 15, corner Calle 46, corner Calle 47 and corner Calle 54.*

TALLER DE CERÁMICAS ARTISTAS

Ceramics made by artists. You can often see them working at night in the lights of their studio. *Av. 1a/C/ 64 | daily 9am–4pm*

SPORTS & ACTIVITIES

PARACHUTING

Glide down like a bird to the coast below– contact the *Aeroclub (Via Blanca, km 31.5 | tel. 45 66 72 56)* to organise a jump. Tandem flights together with experts are offered for beginners *(from 160 CUC).*

JEEP & BOAT SAFARI

The one-day excursion (can be booked in the hotels) takes you to the *Playa Coral* (for snorkelling), *Cueva Saturno* (close to the airport), a cenote (a lake formed from a collapsed sinkhole) where you can take a dip and the INSIDER TIP Río Canímar (near Matanzas) where you can sail by boat to a ranch (offering lunch and horseback riding).

DANCING

Learn the steps of Salsa, Rumba, Mambo, Danzón and Cha-Cha-Cha from Cuban dancers at the *abc academia baile en cuba (Av. 1ra/C/ 34 | daily 9am, 11.30am, 2.30pm and 5.30pm),* private lessons also available *(2 hours/15 CUC).*

DIVING

Well-trained diving instructors, attractive diving spots: *Atlantis Varadero (Autopista Sur, km 15 | www.scubaatlantisvaradero.com)* is the right address for both beginners and advanced divers.

ENTERTAINMENT

LA BAMBA

The DJ plays sounds of salsa, pop and rock to get people onto the dancefloor at this legendary hotel disco. *Hotel Tuxpan | Av. de las Américas | tel. 45 66 75 60 | daily from 11pm | admission 10 CUC*

BAR CALLE 62

Live music, cocktails, light snacks and especially the prominent corner location in Varadero's small amusement quarter have made this bar the top meeting place. *Daily 8am–2am | Av. 1ra/C/ 62 | tel. 45 66 81 67*

THE BEATLES

A crowd magnet especially when the bar organises its live open-air concerts. Take a selfie with the life-size iconic Beatles cast in bronze to round off the fun. *Av. 1ra/Calle 59 | Eintritt frei*

WHERE TO STAY

Around 50 large hotels (mainly with all-inclusive deals) are spread over the Hicacos peninsula, starting at Punta Arenas in the west to Punta Francés in the east. The fanciest establishments can be found on the eastern part of the peninsula, including several *Meliá* and *Iberostar* resorts *(www.melia.com | www.iberostar.com).* There are a few state-owned hotels such as the *Dos Mares* or the *Pullman Hotel* (both *www.islazul.cu)* at the heart of the resort and a few privately-run accommodations *(casas particulares).*

MANSIÓN XANADÚ ★

The marble baths with art nouveau and art deco taps, which the patron owner of the villa, American industrial magnate DuPont de Nemours , just couldn't resist in 1930, can be enjoyed by hotel guests these days. Accommodation rates include breakfast and the green fee for the golf course. Housed in the former library is the *Las Américas* restaurant *(daily noon–4pm, 7pm–9.30pm | Expensive)* ,

colonial-style hotel resort in the centre. *160 rooms on the beach, 122 in terraced bungalows | 1ra Av. | betw. C/ 60 and 64 | tel. 45 66 70 40 | www.starfishresorts. com | Moderate*

Musical accompaniment at the Paradisus Varadero Hotel

the top-floor bar ☀ *El Mirador Casa Blanca (daily 10am–11pm)* offers spectacular views. *6 rooms | Ave. Las Américas, km 8.5 | tel. 45 66 73 88 | www.varadero-golfclub.com | Expensive*

PARADISUS VARADERO
A solitary bay, delightful stretch of sand and first-class hotel: This five-star all-inclusive resort offers a selection of suites, villas with private pool and family concierge rooms tailored to the needs of families with children. Wedding and honeymoon packages are also available. *794 rooms | Punta Francés | tel. 45 66 87 00 | www.melia.com | Expensive*

QUATRO PALMAS
The former private villa of Dictator Batista is integrated into this delightful

VILLA MARGARITA
Do you like the quiet life? Then this villa surrounded by a delightful garden is perfect for you. It is just ten minutes on foot to the beach. *3 rooms | C/ 22 and 3ra Ave. | tel. 45 61 42 12 | Budget*

WICHO & KAREN
Small, privately-owned oasis at the heart of Varadero with a pretty garden. Situated slightly away from the main road, this accommodation is still in close proximity to the beach. When booking a reservation, guests are asked to pay an advance deposit for one night. *4 rooms | C/ 54 Nr. 103. betw. Av. 1ra/2da | tel. 45 61 49 24 | wichokaren96@gmail. com | Budget*

CUBATUR

This agency offers a professional and extremely friendly service. The bright members of staff can organise regional excursions for you and can even reserve rooms in private accommodation for the next stage of your journey. *C/ 33/1ra Av. | tel. 45 66 72 17 | www.cubatur.cu*

WHERE TO GO

CÁRDENAS
(130 C2) (ØØ F2)

Situated 15 km/9 miles southeast from Varadero, the town (pop. 100,000) is worth visiting for its unvarnished Cuban flair. It's also worth visiting the INSIDERTIP *Museo Oscar María de Rojas (Plaza San José | Echeverría | Tue–Sat 10am–6pm, Sun 9am–noon | guided tour 5 CUC),* with its baroque-style funeral carriage and other interesting cultural and natural artefacts from Cuba.

LOW BUDGET

Ply all hotels and beaches of Varadero all day long for only 5 CUC? It's possible with the *hop-on-hop-off* buses. And the Matanzas–Varadero day ticket is only 10 CUC.

Don't be afraid of internet bookings: if you want to take advantage of cheap all-inclusive hotels, you'll have to comb their websites or the major travel bookings portals (e.g. *www.booking.com* or *www.galahotels.com*) for special deals – they're only available online!

CAYO LARGO ★ (130 B–C5) *(ØØ E–F4)*

This is the southernmost of a number of islets between the Zapata peninsula and the Isla de la Juventud: Cayo Largo covers only 15 sq miles *(only accessible by air, as a day trip from Varadero).* Many reckon this to be the most beautiful spot on Cuba, because the Caribbean Sea is so present here, the beach so white and as long as the entire island: 25 km/15 miles. If you'd prefer a sand bank for your sunbathing, take a boat across to *Playa Sirena.* The *sea turtle farm* run by biologists is also worth a visit *(daily 9am–6pm | admission 2 CUC).* Ferries also serve the palm-fringed beach of *Avalos*, the iguana island of *Cayo Iguana,* the snorkelling paradises of *Cayo Rico* and the sea-bird colony of *Cayo Pájaro.* The most luxurious hotel on the island is the *Sol Cayo Largo (296 rooms | tel. 45 24 82 60 | www.melia. com | Expensive).* The 53 palm-covered beach cabañas of the *Villa Lindamar hotel (tel. 45 24 81 11 | Moderate)* occupy a nice location on the edge of the hotel zone. Info: *www.cayolargodelsur.cu*

CIÉNAGA DE ZAPATA ★
(130 B–C3) (ØØ E–F3)

Cuba's most important wetlands in ecological terms stretch across the Ciénaga de Zapata peninsula and are criss-crossed by rivers and lagoons. Its dense mangrove vegetation provides a habitat for rare water birds and plants. The entrance to this enormous area is *La Boca* at the *Laguna del Tesoro:* with restaurants, souvenir shops and a *crocodile breeding station (daily 9.30am–5pm | admission 5 CUC)* where you can get a close-up look at these scary creatures. More importantly, speed boats also depart from here to *Guamá* (see p. 110), a preserved native Indian village with the stilt hotel *Villa Guamá (44 rooms | tel. 45 91 55 51 | www.cubanacan.cu | Budget–*

Moderate) which has become slightly dated in appearance.

GIRÓN/BAHÍA DE COCHINAS
(130 C3–4) (*⊕ F3*)

Deep in the south of the Matanzas province (which includes Varadero), the famous *Bahía de Cochinas* (Bay of Pigs) cuts deep into the land, flanked by the

MATANZAS (130 B2) (*⊕ E–F2*)

The view of the pretty curved bay of Matanzas, 30 km/18 miles west of Varadero, quickly captivates visitors to the capital (pop. 150,000) of the Matanzas province. The small centre of the former sugar port boasts old palaces such as the *Palacio del Junco,* where the comprehensive *Museo Histórico Provincial (C/ Milanés | betw. 272

Fighter plane at the Museo de la Intervención in the Bay of Pigs

Ciénaga de Zapata, and towards the Caribbean coast the wild Playa Girón with the village of *Girón.* This is where mercenaries hired by exiled Cubans landed in 1961, in order to liberate Cuba from communism. The *Museo de la Intervención (daily 8am–5pm | 2 CUC)* and 48 stone monuments for the fallen commemorate the failed invasion. Hotel: *Playa Girón (287 rooms | tel. 45 98 41 10 | Budget).* The water in the rock basins of INSIDER TIP *Caleta Buena (daily 10am–5pm | 15 CUC incl. drinks and food)* 8 km/5 miles east of Playa Girón runs crystal clear.

and 274 | Tue–Sat 9am–5pm, Sun 9am–noon | admission 2 CUC)* documents all periods. Diagonally across, the *Teatro Sauto* (1863, *Plaza de Vigía*) is a testimony to the sugar barons' appreciation of the arts at the time. Calle 83 leads directly to the old *Triolet* pharmacy, today the *Museo Farmacéutico (C/ 83 no. 4951 | Mon–Sat 9am–6pm, Sun 10am–2pm | admission 3 CUC),* a feast for the eyes of retro lovers. Attractions outside the city include the *Cuevas de Bellamar* (see p. 110), the *Río Canimar (boat trips from 30 CUC)* and the nearby *Tropicana open-air stage (Autopista Varadero, km 4.5 | tel. 45 26 53 80 | advance ticket sales in the Varadero hotels).*

THE CENTRE

The heart of Cuba sits like a buffer between cosmopolitan Havana to the west and Caribbean-feel Santiago to the east: a quiet and rural region with the Carretera Central as its main artery interspersed by the towns of Santa Clara, Ciego de Ávila and Camagüey. The small roads leading down to the coast are all the more surprising.

The first of these is north of the turbulent university town of Santa Clara where Che Guevara helped the revolution to victory: a long dam stretches along the coast and across the sea to the offshore Cayos Ensenachos, Las Brujas and Santa María and their holiday resorts. There is another dam to the north of Ciego de Avila running from the coast far out to offshore islands once called *Jardines del Rey,*

or King's Garden, in honour of the Spanish king. The largest of these islands are the holiday paradises Cayo Coco and Cayo Guillermo which even have their own airport. However these are the only two inhabited outcrops among the staggering number of many tiny *cayos* (islands) and reefs of both archipelagos bordering Central Cuba in the North, otherwise known as Cayería del Norte. The last of these isles to the north of Camagüey near Playa Santa Lucía are popular for diving trips and excursions. The attractions of Central Cuba's north coast are hidden behind the Escambray, a range of mountains with dams and waterfalls: namely its Caribbean coastal towns steeped in history such as the perfectly preserved Spanish colonial Trinidad, a World Heritage Site, as is the

Cayos and colonial atmosphere: experience nature and water sports, or take an inspiring stroll on the historic cobbles of an old quarter

centre of the neighbouring Cienfuegos with its noble villa district Punta Gorda.

CAMAGÜEY

(133 D3) *(K4)* **With its winding streets (to protect against pirate invasion) and plethora of old churches, colonial squares, artists and writers, Camagüey is known for going its own way. Camagüey (pop. 330,000) was declared a World Heritage Site by Unesco in 2008.**

> **WHERE TO START?**
> **Plaza de los Trabajadores:** The name "Labourers Square" is a bit misleading. This might be where Camagüey's heart beats, yet more in the sense of creativity and zest for life. Start off with great art in the Casa de Cultura (blue building), and browse the small stalls and shops in nearby Calle Maceo. The latter leads into República, where you'll find all the important agencies.

The city's symbol are *tinajones*, large terracotta jars once used by the wealthy to collect rainwater in the rainy season. Diego Velázquez founded the city on the coast in 1514, giving it the name Santa María Puerto Príncipe. It was moved in 1516 to the banks of the Río Caonao and

entrance fee goes to securing the future of this famous ballet company. You can also wander around the dressmakers and the shoe menders. Book your tickets at the *Paradiso Agency (Calle Ignacio Agramonte 409 | tel. 32 28 60 59 | www. paradisonline.com)*. More information is

Lifelike couple: bronze sculpture by Martha Jiménez on the Plaza del Carmen

in 1528 further inland. In 1923, Camagüey received the name it bears today, taken from the cacique Camagüebax. The city is famous for its cultural life. It is home to the poet Nicolás Guillén (1902–89) and the freedom fighter Ignacio Agramonte (1841–73). *www.ohcamaguey.cu*

SIGHTSEEING

INSIDER TIP ▶ BALLET DE CAMAGÜEY/ CAMAQUITO

A great event put on especially for tourists: Take the opportunity to watch the virtuosity of these young ballet pupils during a special performance in the practice hall of the Camagüey ballet school. The event is also for a good cause: your

available from Mark Kuster at the *Camaquito aid project (tel. 32 27 01 57)*.

MUSEO CASA NATAL DE IGNACIO AGRAMONTE

Jugs *(tinajones)* on the patio, antique furniture and historic documentation in the birth house of Ignacio Agramonte (1841–71) remind visitors of this prolific revolutionary who died fighting in the first war of independence against the Spanish. *Av. Agramonte 459 | Mon–Sat 9am–4.45pm, Sun until 2.30pm | admission 2 CUC*

PLAZA DEL CARMEN

Splendid plaza with the Iglesia de Nuestra Señora del Carmen (1825) and the "gossiping" bronze statues by Martha

Jiménez. You are invited to take a break at *El Ovejito (daily noon–midnight | tel. 32 24 24 98 | Budget–Moderate)*; speciality is the lamb (as the name suggests). *Herm. Agüero | betw. C/ Homda/Carmen*

PLAZA SAN JUAN DE DIOS
The pretty colonial square is framed by merchants' houses with restaurants and the INSIDER TIP gallery of artist couple Joel Jover and Ileana Sánchez *(conojo degato.blogspot.com)* as well as the *Antiguo Hospital de Dios*, once a hospital (1728), today the *Museum of Colonial Architecture (Tue–Sat 9am–5pm, Sun 9am–1pm | admission 1 CUC)*, with great views from its ↘ mirador.

FOOD & DRINK

CAFÉ CIUDAD
Trendy coffee shop on the former Plaza de Armas, now Plaza Agramonte; good sandwiches, cool cocktails. *Daily 9am–11pm | Plaza Agramonte/Cisneros | tel. 32 25 84 12 | Budget–Moderate*

INSIDER TIP CASA AUSTRIA/CAFÉ SISSI
A touch of Austria in the Caribbean. The confectioner and solicitor Sepp (originally from the Salzburg region) offers guests Wiener schnitzel, goulash and other sweet Austrian specialities. The casa also houses three comfortable rooms *(Budget)*. *Daily 7.30am–11.30pm | C/ Lugareño 121/betw. San Rafael/San Clemente | tel. 32 28 55 80 | Budget–Moderate*

ENTERTAINMENT

LA BIGORNIA
On weekends great atmosphere and live music *(Fri–Sun from 9pm)* from salsa to Latin Jazz. Two blocks from the Hotel *Colón* in the pedestrian precinct. *República 394 | tel. 3 22 47 84*

WHERE TO STAY

COLÓN
Unadulterated nostalgia rules, from the bar in the lobby to the furniture and the 47 comfortable rooms; the hotel first opened in 1926. *Av. República 472 | betw. San José/San Martín | tel. 32 25 48 78 | www.islazul.cu | Moderate*

E GRAN HOTEL
You won't find more central and better accommodation in Camagüey: built in 1939, the hotel has a good restaurant, a pool and a roof terrace. *72 rooms | C/ Maceo 67 | tel. 32 29 20 93 | Expensive*

PUCHY
The proprietor Puchy and his wife are discrete and helpful hosts. Their house lies in a quiet side road in the centre (with parking space). *3 separate rooms | C/ San Antonio 70 | betw. C/ Martí/Agüero | tel. 32 29 33 17 | Budget*

★ **Cayo Coco**
A wild island and dream hotels
→ p. 68

★ **Museo Memorial del Ernesto Che Guevara**
Pilgrimage site in Santa Clara for all fans of the never-forgotten revolutionary → p. 70

★ **Palacio de Valle**
Visit the palace and enjoy crayfish between Moorish mosaics in Cienfuegos → p. 66

★ **Trinidad**
Fine views from the tower of the city museum across the heritage old quarter → p. 72

MARCO POLO HIGHLIGHTS

PLAYA SANTA LUCÍA (133 F3) *(L–M4)*
A beautiful long beach (21 km/13 miles) with a few resorts and in the back a lagoon with flamingos – that's Playa Santa Lucía (110 km/68 miles from Camagüey). This small resort in the fishing village *La Boca* has an authentic Caribbean feel. The privately-run *Hostal Coco Beach (3 rooms | house 6 | tel. 0 52 48 93 59 | Budget)* lies on the sea front and in walking distance

cosmopolitan ease of a port, the confidence of an industrial centre and a pinch of French flair brought over by settlers from the French colony of Louisiana.

The provincial capital (pop. 160,000) lies in a deep bay, which since 1745 has been protected by the *Castillo de Jagua*. Founded in 1819, and soon connected to the Cuban railway network, it rose from the mid-19th century to be the most important sugar port in the south. The city's former wealth is reflected in the villas

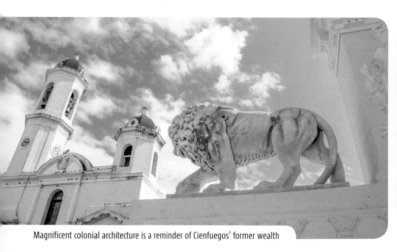

Magnificent colonial architecture is a reminder of Cienfuegos' former wealth

to the enchanting palm beach *Playa de los Cocos.* Divers come here for its amazing reefs and (between Nov. and March) to feed the INSIDER TIP habituated sharks. The diving centre is *Marlin Santa Lucía (tel. 32 36 5182 | www.nauticamarlin.com)* at the *Brisas Santa Lucía (400 rooms | tel. 32 33 6140 | www.hotelescubanacan. com | Moderate–Expensive)*.

on the Punta Gorda peninsula and the Paseo El Prado boulevard. The historic centre entered the Unesco list of World Heritage sites in 2004. A worthwhile excursion for nature lovers is the *El Nicho* waterfall in the nearby Escambray mountains.

CIENFUEGOS

(131 D4) *(G3)* **Cienfuegos, the "Pearl of the South", receives visitors with the**

PALACIO DE VALLE ★
Gothic, Napoleonic neo-classical and Moorish elements come together in this opulent villa, built between 1913 and 1917 for the Asturian-born sugar baron Acisclo

del Valle Blanco. Superb views from the ⚜ rooftop terrace *(Mirador bar daily 10am–11pm)*. Today, the Palacio belongs to the *Hotel Jagua (149 rooms | C/ 37 no. 1 | Punta Gorda | tel. 43 55 10 03 | Moderate–Expensive)* as well as its overpriced restaurant on the groound floor *(daily 10am–11pm | Moderate–Expensive)*.

PARQUE MARTÍ

Generously laid-out, with a bandstand, surrounded by magnificent restored houses, the park is home to the classicist *Teatro Tomás Terry* (1890), the *Palacio Ferrer* with ⚜ viewing tower, the *Museo Provincial (1893, Tue–Sat 10am–6pm, Sun 9am–noon | admission 2 CUC)*, documenting the history of the city, as well as the *cathedral* (19th century).

CLUB CIENFUEGOS ⚜

Terrace with splendid views of the bay, international cuisine on the ground floor *(daily noon–3pm | Expensive)*, on the first floor the *Café Cienfuegoes (until 9.30pm)*, with live music occasionally. *C/ 37 | betw. C/ 8/12 | Punta Gorda | tel. 43 51 28 91 | Expensive*

INSIDER TIP FINCA DEL MAR ⚜

Sophisticated location with stylishly decorated terrace overlooking the bay. Creative cuisine which only uses the freshest ingredients. *Daily noon–midnight | C/ 35 | betw. C/ 18/20 | Punta Gorda | tel. 43 52 65 98 | Moderate–Expensive*

ENTERTAINMENT

CLUB EL BENNY

Great sounds of disco music and live performance bands. Cabaret is sometimes performed at the disco (check out the posters). *Ave. 54 | pedestrian zone, betw.*

29/31 | tel. 43 55 11 05 | daily 10pm–1am | admission from 4 CUC

WHERE TO STAY

INSIDER TIP HOSTAL BAHÍA ⚜

In Diana and Omar's beautiful *casa particular* you'll be living with a view of the bay. The house is decorated with works by a Cuban artist. *2 rooms (en-suite, safe) | Ave. 20 no. 3502 | corner 35 | Altos | hostalbahia@yahoo.es | Budget*

PALACIO AZUL

The "blue palace" next to the yacht club gives you large rooms with sat-TV and safe, plus a good restaurant and bar. *7 rooms | C/ 37 no. 1201 | betw. 12/14 | tel. 43 55 58 29 | www.gran-caribe.com | Moderate*

LA UNIÓN

Cienfuegos' best city hotel is situated near the Bulevar, the Parque Martí and

LOW BUDGET

Souvenir shoppers can hunt for a bargain Tue–Sun between 8am and 5pm at the crafts market on *Plaza San Juan de Dios* in Camagüey.

● Every morning from 10am, the large flight of steps leading up to the *Casa de Música (C/ Juan Manuel Márquez)* next to the *Iglesia Parroquial de la Santísima Trinidad* in Trinidad hosts free live music; show from 10pm.

For only 5 CUC you can use the *hop-on-hop-off* buses on the route between Trinidad and the pretty Playa Ancón all day long between 9am and 7pm.

the Prado *(Calle 37)*. Elegant rooms, a courtyard pool and a popular rooftop bar. *49 rooms | C/ 31/54 | tel. 43 55 10 20 | www.hotellaunion-cuba.com | Moderate*

WHERE TO GO

JARDÍN BOTÁNICO (131 D–E4) *(G3)*
Exotic variety of magnificent tropical plants: 300 types of palms, 23 kinds of bamboo, all in all some 2,000 local and foreign plants can be seen in the botanical gardens founded in 1901 by American sugar magnate Edwin F. Atkins in collaboration with Harvard University. Restaurant and cafeteria. *Ctra. a Trinidad Central Pepito Tey | daily 8am–4.30pm | admission 2.50 CUC*

PLAYA RANCHO LUNA
(131 D4) *(G3)*
Long white sandy beach between the hotels *Club Amigo Rancho Luna (222 rooms | all inclusive | tel. 43 54 80 12 | Expensive)* and the quieter *Faro Luna (46 rooms | tel. 43 54 80 30 | Moderate)*, both a good 14 km/8 miles south of the city on the Carretera Pasacaballo *(both: www.grancaribe.cu)*. There are a few *casas particulares* in front of the Faro hotel; the beach is freely accessible.

JARDINES DEL REY

(132–133 C–D1) *(J–K 2–3)* **Those who don't touch down at the international airport of Cayo Coco can reach this central group of islands of the Archipiélago Sabana-Camagüey via Morón by car across a 17 km/11 mile causeway *(pedraplén)*.**

At the barrier of the connecting causeway, you'll have to pay 2 CUC (and the same again on the way back) and show your passport. The 140 sq mile main island of ★ *Cayo Coco* has most of the hotels. To the east, bridges and causeways connect it with *Cayos Romano* and *Paredón Grande*, as yet unexploited by tourism, as well as to the west with *Cayo Guillermo* (5 sq miles). The islands are said to have been given the name of *Jardines del Rey* ("Garden of the King") by Diego de Velázquez. Today, the island chain belongs to the Buenavista biosphere reserve. Away from the hotels, mangrove swamps and shrub forests shelter 360 kinds of plants and 200 endemic animal species, including the white ibis or *coco,* as the Cubans call this bird (hence the name of the island, *Cayo Coco*).

SIGHTSEEING

PARQUE NATURAL EL BAGÁ
(132 C1) *(ᗰ J3)*
Do not be put off by the seemingly neglected entrance to this park. The network of trails through this 7.6 km^2 / 4.7 miles^2 unspoilt area (forest, lakes, mangrove coast) is accessible to all visitors. Guides are usually waiting at the side entrance to show you around. The price depends on your bartering skills. *Ctra. a Cayo Guillermo, km 11 | Cayo Coco*

FOOD & DRINK

SITIO LA GÜIRA
This settlement offers visitors a glimpse of how people once lived on the islands: living as charcoal burners in huts with hens and pigs. The restaurants at this reconstructed site serve hearty Cuban dishes. INSIDER TIP Basic cabañas *(25 CUC/night)* are also rented. *Daily 9am–11pm | Cayo Coco | Ctra. a Cayo Guillermo, km 10 | tel. 33 30 12 08 | Budget*

SPORTS & BEACHES

At the ● *Acuavida Spa Talaso (Av. de los Hoteles | tel. 0 53 64 76 76)* you can enjoy a massage and a choice of many other treatments outdoors on the cliffs. All larger hotels offer a wide variety of sporting and fitness activities. Kite surfers meet up at the *Hotel Sol Cayo Guillermo (www.kite-cuba.com, www.melia.com).* Of the nine beaches on Cayo Coco and three on Cayo Guillermo, INSIDER TIP *Playa Pilar* (named after Hemingway's ship "Pilar" which often sailed by) on Cayo Guillermo is the most beautiful. Catamaran sailors will take you to the *Cayo Media Luna,* where Batista had a summer residence, or for a snorkelling trip to the reef. One of the dishes served at the restaurant *(daily 9am–5pm | Budget–Moderate)* is crayfish for 15 CUC *(bus stop on the hop-on-hop-off tour)*.

WHERE TO STAY

The Cayos are enclaves for all-inclusive tourism; there is no privately-owned accommodation on the islands. Last minute guests can sometimes reserve a room at the 24-hour Cubatur booth in front of the barrier.

APARTHOTEL AZUL

No-frills hotel with apartment blocks catering for business travellers, workers and short-staying visitors. Large common pool with restaurant bar. *30 apartments | Ctra. a Cayo Guillermo, km 1,5 | tel. 33 30 81 21 | www.islazul.cu | Moderate*

COLONIAL

Tourism on Cayo Coco all started at this "colonial" hotel village. A plaque marks its unveiling by Fidel Castro in 1993. Has been modernised several times since it opened. *458 rooms | tel. 33 30 13 11 | www.cubanacan.cu | Expensive*

WHERE TO GO

CIEGO DE ÁVILA (132 C2) *(J3–4)*

After a long drive along the Carretera Central it's worth taking a break here. Named after its first landowner Jacome de Avila, this provincial capital (pop. 150,000) has been revamped with an amusement park yet fortunately remains unspoilt by tourism (many CUP

Enough space for everyone: endless beaches on Cayo Coco

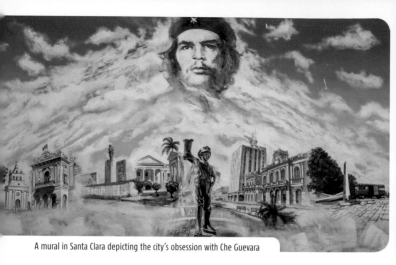

A mural in Santa Clara depicting the city's obsession with Che Guevara

locals). The Indian archaeological finds are worth seeing in the *Museo Provincial (Tue–Sat 9am–5pm, Sun 8am–noon | admission 1 CUC)*. Next door stands the well-kept private accommodation *Yolanda (2 rooms | C/ Independencia Oeste 317 | tel. 3 33 38 45 | Budget)*.

MORÓN (132 C2) *(J3)*

Surrounded by sugar-cane fields and lagoons, the town 59 km/36 miles south of Cayo Coco is is a good base for excursions out to the islands. A sculpture of a rooster is a reminder of the Andalusian origin of the first settlers. Pretty train station building (1923), good *casas particulares*, e.g. the *Casa Colonial Carmen (C/ General Peraza 38 | betw. Felipe/ Céspedes | tel. 33 50 54 53 | casacarmen. cubarentaroom.com | Budget)*.

SANTA CLARA

(132 A1) *(∭ H3)* **The provincial capital (pop. 240,000) is where Che Guevara waged the final battle against Batista's** soldiers to win victory. It is no surprise then that this university town plays special homage to this special *guerillero*.

Founded in 1691 by inhabitants of nearby Remedios, *Santa Clara* quickly grew into an important centre for the tobacco and sugar industry and a railway line to Havana was built in 1873. Today the city is the gateway to the Cayos Santa María.

MONUMENTO A LA TOMA Y ACCIÓN DEL TREN BLINDADO ●

Original wagons of the armoured train which was derailed by the rebels on 29 December 1958 on Che Guevara's orders, in order to force Batista's locked-in soldiers to surrender. *Av. de Libaración/C/ Camajuani | Tue–Sat 5.30pm | admission 1 CUC*

MUSEO MEMORIAL DEL ERNESTO CHE GUEVARA ★ ●

This memorial was erected in 1988 to commemorate the 30th anniversary of Che Guevara's victory over the Batista troops on 31 December 1958 in this town. In 1997, the revolutionary's mortal remains, transferred from Bolivia, found their last resting place here. The exhibition includes Che's farewell letter and the passport he used to enter Bolivia. *Av. de los Defiles/Circunvalación | Tue–Sun 9.30am–5pm | admission free*

FOOD & DRINK

CASA DEL GOBERNADOR

The pretty colonial house, the gem of the boulevard (pedestrian zone) is again the best restaurant around. Large menu, reservation recommended. *Daily 8am–10.45pm | C/ Independencia/corner Zayas | tel. 42 20 22 73 | Budget–Moderate*

WHERE TO STAY

LA CASA DE ERNESTO Y MIREYA

This *casa particular* offers quiet, first-floor rooms in a lovingly looked after house. Serves filling breakfasts! *3 rooms | C/ Cuba 227 (altos) | betw. C/ Síndico/Pastora | tel. 42 27 35 01 | Budget*

LOS CANEYES

For those who like to stay in natural surroundings outside the city: this resort, designed in Indian style, offers a pool, bar and disco. *95 rooms/bungalows | Av. de los Eucaliptos | tel. 42 21 81 40 | www.hotelloscaneyes.com | Moderate*

WHERE TO GO

CAYO LAS BRUJAS (132 B1) (*Ⓜ J2–3*)

"Witches' island" is named after the local legend of two unfortunate lovers. Today, couples fall in love with the hotel *Villa Las Brujas (23 rooms | access to the left of the airport | tel. 42 35 00 24 | Moderate)* situated in the middle of a wild garden next to a splendid beach.

INSIDER TIP Day guests can dine in the hotel's restaurant for 15 CUC.

CAYO SANTA MARÍA (132 C1) (*Ⓜ J3*)

Your only company on this remote offshore island are the sea and the skies – if you overlook the many all-inclusive hotels *(all Expensive)*. These include four resorts belonging to the hotel group *Meliá (www.melia.com)*, a family-friendly *Memories Resort (www.memoriesresorts.com)* and the *Husa Cayo Santa María (1308 junior suites | www.gaviota-grupo.com)*. Right next door is the artistic village *Pueblo de Estrella*. Similar to *Pueblo de las Dunas* (next to *Meliá de la Dunas)*, it offers souvenir markets, restaurants and exchange offices. What's left of nature has been squeezed into the *Refugio de Fauna y Flora*, a small paradise for birdwatchers *(daily 9am–5pm | admission 4 CUC)*.

REMEDIOS (132 A1) (*H3*)

Visit this town at the weekends for the brass band concert held ● every Sunday in the attractive colonial centre! Its foundation date of 1514 makes Remedios one of Cuba's oldest towns. Remedios can also boast one of the most beautiful churches in Latin America: the altar of the **INSIDER TIP** *Catedral San Juan Bautista (1692)* is entirely gilded. Also worth seeing is the *Museo de las Parrandas (C/ Alejandro del Río 74 | daily 9am–noon, 1pm–5pm | guided tour 1 CUC, photo 5 CUC)* with costumes from the town's fireworks and costume festival *(16/24 Dec)*. Reside in style at the *Hotel Mascotte (10 rooms | C/ Máximo Gómez 114 | Moderate)* on the main square, at the *E Barcelona (24 rooms | C/ José A. Peña 67 | booking for both at tel. 42 39 51 44 45 | Moderate)* or in the private palace of *La Casona Cueto (9 rooms | Alejandro del Rio 72 | betw. E. Malaret/Máximo Gómez | tel. 42 39 53 50 | Budget)*.

TRINIDAD

(131 E4) *(H4)* **Cobbled streets, high wooden doors with iron grilles for "whispering secrets", low tiled roofs and baroque churches transport visitors back to colonial times in ★ Trinidad.**

Founded by Diego Velázquez in 1514, the city (pop. 50,000) became rich at the start of the 19th century during the sugar boom. The liberation of the slaves and the War of Independence stopped the town's development short and the port lost its importance. Declared a Unesco World Heritage site in 1989, Trinidad is one of Cuba's most important tourist attractions today, together with the *Valle de los Ingenios*, the valley of the sugar factories, in the town's hinterland. In the south behind the mouth of the Río Guaurabo at La Boca (variety of private accommodation available), you can bathe at the beautiful 4 km/2.5 mile-long beach of the Ancón peninsula *(shuttle bus 9am–6pm from Cubatur office | C/ Antonio Maceo/Zerquera | admission 5 CUC)*. The holiday resort *Las Brisas (241 rooms | tel. 41 99 65 00 | Expensive)* offers an all-inclusive holiday.

SIGHTSEEING

MUSEO MUNICIPAL ☆

Richly adorned with stucco and frescoes, the former house of the sugar baron Cantero is today the city museum. The patio was once used for cooking and from the top of the tower you have spectacular panoramic views. *C/ Simón Bolívar 423 | daily 9am–5pm | admission 2 CUC*

MUSEO ROMÁNTICO ●

Excess of luxury: The former palace of the Conde Brunet shows the luxuries of the sugar aristocracy. *C/ F. H. Echerri 52/* *Simón Bolívar | Tue–Sat 9am–5pm, Sun 9am–1pm | admission 2 CUC*

VALLE DE LOS INGENIOS

Aka "valley of horrors" where slaves were once worked to death in the sugar mills by their merciless guards. Built in 1816, the 43 m/141 ft high guard tower *(admission 2 CUC)* in *Manaca Iznaga* can still be seen. Why not take a gentle trundle on the ● *tren de vapor* (steam train) through the sugar-cane fields *(daily from 9.30am from Estación de Toro in Trinidad | 10 CUC)?*

FOOD & DRINK

LA CANCHÁNCHARA

Cosy meeting place for lovers of the eponymous drink made from honey, rum and lemon juice. *Daily 10am–8pm | C/ Rubén Martínez Villena 78 | Budget*

INSIDER TIP QUINCE CATORCE

Fine dining in a museum setting: This residence has been in the possession of one family since 1514 who now share this old grandeur with visitors. *Daily noon–4pm and from 6.30pm | C/ Simón Bolívar 515 | tel. 41 99 42 55 | Moderate–Expensive*

SHOPPING

LA CASA DEL ALFARERO

Long-established ceramics workshop. The masks painted in Santería colours make pretty souvenirs. *Andrés Berro 9 | betw. Avel Santamaría/Julio A. Mella*

WHERE TO STAY

CASAS PARTICULARES

Good private accommodation: hostal *Doctora Margarita (C/ Simón Bolívar 113 | betw. P. Zerquera/A. Cárdenas | tel. 41 99 32 26 | Budget)*, and the *Casa Colonial Carlos*

(*Lino Pérez 212/betw. Frank País/Miguel Calzada | tel. 41 99 32 50 | 0 52 90 99 08 | Budget*).

LAS CUEVAS ☆

Magnificent views across town and bay, museum cave and the `INSIDER TIP` *cave disco Ayala (Tue–Sun from 10pm)*. The hotel lies on a slope behind the town. *109 rooms | Finca Santa Ana | tel. 41 99 61 33 | rwww.hotelescubanacan.com | Moderate*

m/2,600 ft) into a world of waterfalls, valleys and gentle heights supporting cedar, pine, teak, agnolia and mahogany trees, ferns, blossoms, hummingbirds and butterflies. Pick up trail maps and hiking guides from the information centre *(daily 8am–5pm)* in front of the *Escambray spa hotel (www.gaviota-grupo.com)*.

SANCTI SPÍRITUS (131 F4) *(H3)*

Another colonial gem, 70 km/43.5 miles northeast of Trinidad: The provin-

Once the proud capital of the sugar boom: the 500-year old Trinidad

IBEROSTAR GRAN HOTEL TRINIDAD

Small 5-star oasis for adult guests only in the historic centre, with covered patio; show cooking, games room, internet café. *40 rooms | C/ Jose Martí 262 | betw. Lino Pérez/Colón | tel. 41 99 60 73 | www.iberostar.com | Expensive*

WHERE TO GO

GRAN PARQUE NATURAL TOPES DE COLLANTES (131 F4) *(H4)*

From Trinidad, 18 km/11 miles of hairpin bends lead to Topes de Collantes (800

cial capital (pop. 115,000) was founded in 1514 on the Río Tuinucú and relocated to the Río Yayabo in 1520 where you can cross Cuba's only surviving stone arched bridge. The *Iglesia Parroquial Mayor* can be seen on the Plaza Honorato (built in 1680, splendid ceilings in Mudéjar style). *Mesón de la Plaza (daily 9am–10.30pm | C/ Máximo Gómez 34 | tel. 41 32 85 46 | Budget–Moderate)* welcomes you to dine and *Hostal del Rijo (16 rooms | tel. 41 32 85 88 | www.hoteldelrijo.com | Budget–Moderate)* to spend a night.

THE EAST

The people of eastern Cuba, *Oriente*, are said not to care much about who is governing in Havana and how. Oriente is Fidel Castro's home turf. His cradle stood near the Bahía de Nipe, a region that turns its back on the rest of Cuba, looking out to sea.

Here, a certain lack of submissive spirit has historical roots. In pre-Columbian times already large autonomous cacique (chieftain) empires existed here. Indian cemeteries, over 1,500 years old, and other archaeological sites are evidence of this Taíno civilisation. The colonial age too started in the east: this was where Columbus first stepped ashore, where he planted the oldest still preserved wooden crosses in the soil, on the spot which was later to give rise to the first colonial town

in Cuba, Baracoa. The town became the seat of the governor – until he took a shine to Santiago de Cuba. The first slave ships moored off this coast, where the refugees from Sainte-Domingue, later Haiti, landed, kick-starting Cuba's coffee and sugar economy. Finally, nearly half a millennium after the Spanish had suffocated Indian resistance with the execution of the cacique Hatuey, it became the place where the plans for two revolutions were hatched.

Nature lovers can look forward to beautiful stretches of coastline: west of Santiago de Cuba, at Cuba's highest peak, Pico Turquino, the Sierra Maestra drops down to the steep coast of the Cayman Trough. In the farthest east, mountain ranges have created a coastline characterised by wild

From the birthplace of the country to islands, beaches and bays – from the cradle of the son sound to the "landing place" of the revolution

coves and river estuaries which in the north changes into a landscape of karst mountains, bays and cayos. The main draw of the east, however, remains Santiago de Cuba, the "home of Cuban music ".

BARACOA

(135 F4) (⌕ P6) **The winding access drive via the La Farola mountain road gives an idea of the remoteness of Baracoa (234 km/145 miles from Santiago de Cuba).**

The city is proud to call itself *primera villa* (first town). In 1492, Columbus rammed a wooden cross into the ground which still stands today. Diego de Velázquez also landed in 1511 continuing his colonisation of the Hispaniola and founded here the first town on Cuba. It even served as the island's capital until Velázquez moved to Santiago de Cuba in 1523. Today the town (pop. 82,000) is a centre of fishing, coffee and cocoa growing – and an oasis for nature lovers. The *Finca Duaba (Ctra. Baracoa–Moa, km 3 | daily 8am–7pm, cocoa*

Cocoa beans – the essential ingredient for chocolate

trail 2 CUC) tourist destination provides you with an insight into rural life. There is also a bathing spot close by.

SIGHTSEEING

CATEDRAL DE NUESTRA SEÑORA DE LA ASUNCIÓN

Neatly framed in silver, Columbus' wooden cross (or what is left of it) stands on your left immediately on entering this church (1805) recently restored to pristine condition. Everyone comes to the church, if not to see the cross then for its WiFi hotspot.

FORTIFICATIONS

They once protected the inhabitants against the threat of pirates: the *Fuerte Matachín* (1739) at the entrance to the city which today houses the *Museo Municipal (daily 9am–noon and 2pm – 6pm | admission 1 CUC)*, the *Fuerte de La Punta* (1803) on leaving the city, today a restaurant with the same name *(daily 10am–10pm | tel. 21 64 18 80 | Budget)* – try the **INSIDER TIP** fish with coconut milk! – and the remains of the *Castillo de Seburoco*

(1739) which have been merged into the *El Castillo Hotel (62 rooms | tel. 21 64 18 80 | www.gaviota-grupo.com | Moderate)* which is still a landmark today.

MUSEO ARQUEOLÓGICO "LA CUEVA DEL PARAÍSO"

How did the Taíno, who bitterly fought against the Spaniards under their leader Guamá, once live? This cave museum focuses on this group of indigenous peoples of the Caribbean, showcasing cult artefacts excavated in the region. A 500-year old skull is also on exhibition – could it be the head of Guamá himself? *Daily 8am–5pm | C/ Reparto Paraíso | admission 3 CUC*

FOOD & DRINK

EL BUEN SABOR

The house of good taste – and this is no exaggeration. Their succulent and tender langoustines and shrimps are delicious. Specialities include beans in coconut milk. Nice terrace and subtle background music. *Daily 11am–11pm | Calixto García | tel. 0 52 38 53 09 | Moderate*

INSIDER TIP CASA DEL CACAO

"Filling station" for chocolate lovers on the new boulevard Baracoas. Photos hanging in the shop document cocoa bean production. *Daily 7am–11pm | Maceo 129 | tel. (21) 64 21 25 | Budget*

WHERE TO STAY

CASA ROSI

Centrally located guesthouse with immaculately furnished rooms with bathroom. The ☼ breakfast terrace offers rooftop views out to sea. *3 rooms | C/ Félix Ruenes 6 | tel. 21 64 33 64 | 0 58 54 99 15 | rosi72@nauta.cu | Budget*

VILLA MAGUANA

This small hotel, which will please individualists, occupies a beautiful position on two wild beaches. *16 rooms | Ctra. Baracoa–Moa, km 22 | tel. (21) 64 12 05 | www.gaviota-grupo.com | Budget*

EXCURSIONS

INFOTUR

The team organises a variety of excursions including to the table-top shaped mountain El Yunque. *Mon–Sat 8.30am–4.45pm | C/ Maceo 129 | tel. 21 64 17 81 | www.cubatravel.cu*

WHERE TO GO

GUANTÁNAMO (135 E4) (∅ O6)

Cuba's easternmost provincial capital (pop. 244,000) is no great beauty; still, colonial houses surviving in its core serve as a reminder of its foundation by French refugees from present-day Haiti. The place grew too fast following the establishment, in 1903, of a US base in the Bahía Guantánamo, a good 12 km/7 miles south. Originally limited, the lease has been extended since 1934, indefinitely. The Cuban government is said never to have cashed the annual cheques. Since 2002, the USA have been using its military basis here as a detention camp free from jurisdiction. Excellent views of the bay can be enjoyed from the INSIDER TIP *Mirador La Gobernadora (Ctra. a Baracoa | daily 9am–9pm).* ● Guantánamo also became famous with the song *Guantánamera,* which serenades *guajiras* (women peasants) of the region. The text is based on a poem *Versos Sencillos* ("simple verse") by José Martís.

PARQUE NACIONAL ALEJANDRO DE HUMBOLDT (135 E4) (∅ O–P5)

The park is home to Cuba's star animal, the miniscule Monte Iberia frog which believe it or not is no bigger than your finger nail. But there is a wealth of animal and plant life in this national park, including 90 species of birds and 2000 types of plants. El Indio or other rangers in the information centre *(Ctra. Moa, km*

★ **Finca Mañacas**
The parental estate of Fidel Castro gives deep insights into his youth → p. 79

★ **Casa de Velázquez**
Santiago boasts Cuba's oldest house, today a colonial museum → p. 82

★ **Casa de la Trova**
All the big stars have performed at this music bar in Santiago → p. 84

★ **La Comandancia de La Plata**
The revolutionaries' hideout in the Sierra Maestra is great hiking terrain → p. 86

MARCO POLO HIGHLIGHTS

30, Bahía de Taco) will happily explain the 16 different vegetation zones in the park using the diagrams exhibited in the centre. They also offer guided walks for example to the ☀ INSIDER TIP *Loma de Piedra (10 CUC/pers., 3 hrs)*. Named after the German botanist and explorer Alexander von Humboldt, the 700 km²/270 sq.mile park is part of an even larger protected area: the biosphere reserve *Cuchillas de Toa*. The mission of the environmental organisation *Oroverde* is to promote sustainable tourism.

HOLGUÍN

(134 B–C3) (*ω N5*) **Cuba's green provincial capital. Situated in the Mayabe Valley and protected on all sides by the karst mountains, Holguín (pop. 300,000) is famous for its parks. Its international airport makes it the central hub in the east.**

The city's emblem is the *Loma de la Cruz* mountain. Its summit cross is reached by a set of 461 steps. On 3 May, the INSIDER TIP *Romerías de Mayo*, this becomes a pilgrimage site for many faithful. However, the city shows no sign of excessive piety. People are full of life and open-minded, in particular since Holguín became the gateway to the *Parque Natural Colón* holiday region (Columbus Nature Park), bringing its fair share of tourists into town. Also known as *Costa Verde* and *Costa Esmeralda*, this vacation region stretches across the bays of the northern coast.

SIGHTSEEING

PLAZA CALIXTO GARCÍA
The heart of the city. Here you will find the post office, the *Teatro Eddy Suñol,* the *Museo de Historia Provincial (Calle Frex-* es 198 | Tue–Sat 8am–4.30pm, Sun 8am– noon | admission 2 CUC) with Holguín's landmark symbol, the *hacha* (a cult Indian object) and the *Casa de la Trova*. To the south of the square (around the corner in the Calle Maceo 129) stands the *Museo de Historía Natural Carlos de la Torre (Tue–Sat 9am–5pm, Sun 9am– noon | admission 1 CUC),* famous for its colourful snail shells.

WHERE TO STAY

MIRADOR DE MAYABE ☀
Rustic-style hotel on the karst hill of Mayabe, with the best view across the city; pool, restaurant. Part of the set-up is the INSIDER TIP *Mayabe museum finca. 24 rooms in villas | Alturas de Mayabe, km 8 | tel. 24 42 21 60 | Moderate*

VILLA LIBA
Situated approximately 250 m/820 ft away from Loma de Cruz and 500 m /1,640 ft from Parque Calixto, this 50s-style villa offers tranquil and central accommodation. With car park. *3 en-suite, air-conditioned rooms | Maceo 46/C/ 18 | tel. 24 42 38 23 | Facebook: Hostal Villa Liba | Budget*

INFORMATION

INFOTUR
Edificio Pico Cristal. 1st floor | C/ Libertad/ Martí | tel. 24 42 50 13

WHERE TO GO

BANES (135 D3) (*ω N5*)
Hard to believe that this sleepy outcrop was once in the hands of the United Fruit Company in pre-revolutionary Cuba and was home to an illustrious upper class including the family of the dictator Fulgencio Batista. Fidel Castro also joined

this privileged society when he married the daughter of the major in 1948. A few buildings on the outskirts of town remind visitors of the U.S. Banana Company which left the country in 1959. The cathedral, in which Fidel Castro was married, is still standing (yet the marriage was annulled back in 1953). The *Museo Indocubano Baní (C/ General Marrero 305 | Tue–Sat 9am–5pm, Sun 8am–noon | admission 1 CUC)* situated opposite the church exhibits archaeological finds from the region. You can meet the *historiador* (historian) and photographer Luis Rafael Quiñones here who organises INSIDER TIP guided tours through his "archaeological capital". Accomodation tip: *Colonial Guest House (C/ H no. 1526 | betw. C/ Veguitas/ Franco | tel. 24 80 22 04 | Budget).*

mission 10, photo-/video permit 10 CUC). The estate of Fidel and Raúl's father comprises 26 buildings, amongst them the reconstructed first residence (burnt down in 1954), where Castro was born on 3 August 1926. The room that Fidel shared with brother Raúl is on view, as well as the cockfighting arena.

Life-size native Indian figures in the Aldea Taína near Banes

BIRÁN (134 C4) (*ﾉﾉ N5*)

A good address is the estate of Ángel Castro Argiz (1875–1956) which lies on the outskirts of the small village 66 km/41 miles to the east of Holguín: the ★ *Finca Mañacas (daily 9am–2pm | ad-*

CAYO NARANJO (134 C3) (*ﾉﾉ N5*)

The island in the large "Orange Bay" is a leisure paradise with many facets: shows with dolphins and sea lions at the biggest crowd puller, *Acuario Cayo Naranyo* (see p. 111), pleasure trips by catamaran *(daily 9.15am)* and beaches for picnics and a dip. *Ferry (daily 9am–9pm): Ctra. Guardalavaca, km 48*

INSIDER TIP CAYO SAETÍA
(135 D3–4) (*ﾉﾉ O5*)

The island, connected with the mainland by a causeway, is home to animals including gazelles, buffaloes, ostriches and antelopes living as they would in the wild *(admission 10 CUC | bring your passport!)*. Accommodation at *Hotel Villa*

Cayo Saetía (16 rooms | tel. 24 9 69 00 | Moderate–Expensive).

GIBARA (134 C3) (⏅ N4–5)
A Spanish fort, pretty white colonial houses and a cave on the town's border: Situated 34km/21 northwest of Holguín, this port town (pop. 40,000) belongs to the younger of Cuba's colonial treasures (founded in 1817). Ferries depart three times a day to the tiny *Playa Blanca*. Hotel tip: *Ordoño (27 rooms | C/ J. Peralta | betw. C/ Donato/Independencia | tel. 24 84 44 48 | www.hotelescubanacan.cu | Moderate).*

GUARDALAVACA (134 C3) (⏅ N4–5)
The name Guardalavaca ("look after the cow") might make you think this place might be a tad boring. But it's not that bad, quite the contrary. Currently housing older all-inclusive hotels such as the *Club Amigo Átlantico (742 rooms | Moderate–Expensive)* and *Las Brisas (437 rooms. | tel. 24 43 02 18 | www.cubanacan.cu | Expensive)* there are now plans to revamp this resort with the 5-star resort *Albatros*. Spread along the region's nicest beach, the resort is a good base for a trip to the *Chorro de Maíta (approx. 7 km/4 miles)* along the road to Banes where cemeteries from pre-Columbus and early colonial times were found. Some of the skeletons are exhibited in the *Museo Chorro de Maíta (daily 9.15am–4.30pm | admission 2 CUC).* On the opposite side of the road, the *Aldea Taína (5 CUC)* reconstructs indigenous life in an Indian village.

PARQUE MONUMENTO NACIONAL BAHÍA DE BARIAY (135 D3) (⏅ N5)
16 Indian God statues surrounded by Greek pillars arranged in the shape of a ship's hull commemorate October 29, 1492 when Christoph Columbus first landed on Cuban soil here. The monument in this spacious park was designed by the artist Caridad Ramos Mosquera in 1992. The park (which is signposted) is close to Fray Benito. *Daily 9am–5pm | admission 8 CUC*

PLAYA ESMERALDA (134 C3) (⏅ N4–5)
Just 4 km/2.5 miles west of Guardalavaca lies this beautiful white, sandy beach. Two Meliá hotels *(www.melia.com)* and the diving school *Sea Lovers (tel. 24 3 00 30)* claim it for themselves: the *Sol Río de Luna y Mares (464 rooms | tel. 24 43 00 60 | Moderate–Expensive)* and to the east the luxury ● *Paradisus Río de Oro & Spa (354 rooms | tel. 24 43 00 90 | Expensive)*. A great attraction at the western end of the bay is the `INSIDER TIP` *Los Guanos (daily 8am–4.30pm | admission 3 CUC)* nature reserve with its well-signposted educational trail.

PLAYA PESQUERO (134 C3) (⏅ N4–5)
The white *Playa Pesquero* drops gently towards the turquoise waters of a bay west of the Bahía Naranjo. There are two Gaviota hotels *(www.gaviota-grupo.com)*: the *Playa Pesquero Resort (944 rooms | large spa | tel. 24 305 30 | Expensive)* and the sporty *Playa Costa Verde (480 rooms | gym, kayaks, bikes | tel. 24 350 10 | Expensive)*. To the north, you also have the friendly *Blau Costa Verde (440 rooms | tel. (21) 350 10 | www.blauhotels.com)*.

PLAYA YURAGUNAL
(134 C3) (⏅ N4–5)
Playa Turquesa, east of Playa Pesquero, belongs to the *RIU Turquesa Resort (531 rooms | tel. 24 43 35 40 | www.riu.com | Expensive)*. Nearby, you'll find the information centre of the `INSIDER TIP` *Bioparque Rocazul (tel. 24 308 33 | daily 8.30am–5pm)*. Named after a blue rock that is found here, the park, extending over 2 sq miles to the *Bahía Naranjo*, of-

fers hiking and horse-riding trails *(from 16 CUC/hr)*, a small zoo with crocodiles, ostriches and jutías (cavy-like rodents) and refreshment stops such as the *Finca Monte Bello (daily 8.30am–5pm | Budget)*.

SANTIAGO DE CUBA

(134 C5) *(∅ N6)* **Cuba's equivalent of New Orleans: African and musical influences dominate this old port city (pop. 450,000). Situated on a vast bay, the city's old music bars, narrow streets and authentic Caribbean flair attract visitors.**
The city's narrow estuary towards the Caribbean is well protected: in front, acting like a stopper, lies the small *Cayo Granma* island, and on the cliff the *San Pedro de la Roca del Morro* fort (Unesco world heritage site) guards the entrance as it did during the period of great danger posed by Jamaican pirates. The central meeting point in the city is the *Parque Céspedes*. Buildings with great historic associations

> **WHERE TO START?**
> **Parque Cespedes:** the best starting point for a wander around town. Bank and Infotur office are to the west and east of the cathedral, where you can also park safely for 1 CUC (for the guards). A few paces lead you to the Casa de la Trova, and the always-vibrant Plaza de Dolores is quickly reached on foot too.

face each other here: the city hall, where Fidel Castro once proclaimed the victory of the revolution from the balcony; the splendid *Hotel Casa Granda*, the *Casa de Velázquez*, former residence of the city founder and first island governor Diego Velázquez; and the imposing *cathedral*, where Pope John Paul II held a reconciliation service in 1998.
From 1524 Santiago de Cuba was the capital of the island, yet had to cede the title to Havana as early as 1607. What saved Santiago from falling into insignificance was the revolution on Haiti. At the time, many coffee and sugar farmers fled to

The heart of Santiago de Cuba: the cathedral near Parque Cespedes

The Calle José Saco, Santiago's main shopping street, never sleeps

Santiago de Cuba with their slaves. Their quarter, stretching south of the historical centre across the *Loma del Intendente*, soon became known for the dances and songs of the slaves: performances that earned it the name "Tivoli". In economic terms, Santiago de Cuba and the whole of Cuba benefited from French know-how in cultivating sugar-cane and coffee. The most famous heritage however is music. In the Barrios, you can still watch the original *tumba francesa* which the Haitian settlers brought with them being danced. The city is also known as the cradle of the Son – and the revolution, for Fidel Castro learned at the city's old colonial Jesuit college values such as discipline which were to make him the victor in the Cuban revolution. Whether he abandoned discipline during the exuberant carnival in July, he has never told.

SIGHTSEEING

CASA DE VELÁZQUEZ ★
One look at the wooden grilles of the balcony give the house away as a colonial gem: the Casa Diego Velázquez was built between 1516 and 1522 for Cuba's first governor. The ground floor, which served as the commander's office, still holds the smelting oven for looted gold. The upper storey used to house the private rooms. In this and the house next door, the *Museo del Ambiente Histórico* shows furniture from the 16th to the 19th centuries. *C/ Félix Peña 610 | Parque Céspedes | daily 9am–5pm | admission 2 CUC | Fri 1.30–5pm Peña de Danzón*

CEMENTERIO SANTA IFIGENIA
Crowds of visitors flock to this cemetery ever since the body of Fidel Castro was buried here. The focus of the cemetery is the grave of the poet and hero of the fight for freedom José Martí. This cemetery also holds the tomb of the Bacardí family. *Ave. Crombet | daily 8am–6pm | admission 1 CUC*

ESCALINITA PADRE PICO/ CALLE JESÚS RABI
This pretty, wide set of steps flanked by houses is the most photogenic connec-

tion between the lower town and Tivoli, the old quarter of the French immigrants, and leads straight to *C/ Jesús Rabi* and the *Museo de Lucha Clandestina (C/ Jesús Rabi 1 | Tue–Sun 9am–5pm | admission 1 CUC)* at the corner. The museum in the former police station is dedicated to the 26th of July Movement, commemorating the storming of the *Moncada* barracks. **INSIDER TIP** During his studies in Santiago de Cuba, Fidel Castro lived at Calle Jesús Rabi 6.

FORTALEZA DE SAN PEDRO DE LA ROCA DEL MORRO ☆

This impressive fortification was built between 1638–1700 according to the plans of the military engineer Juan Bautista Antonelli. It was declared a Unesco world heritage site in 1997. The exhibition inside the fortress provides information on filibusters, buccaneers and pirates and you can also see canons, a dungeon and documentation on the Spanish-American naval battle (1898) off the coast of Santiago; the **INSIDER TIP** splendid panoramic view alone is worth the visit. 207 steps lead down to the coast. *Daily 8am–7.30pm | admission 4 CUC*

MUSEO DEL CARNAVAL

Masks, costumes, typical musical instruments such as *congas* and *cornetas*, posters and photos give an idea of Santiago's vibrant carnival (last week in July). *C/ Heredia 303 | Tue–Fri 9am–5pm, Sat 2pm–10pm | folklore performances Tue–Sat 4pm (included in the admission fee) | 1 CUC*

MUSEO HISTÓRICO 26 DE JULIO ●

Before the revolution, the *Moncada* barracks were the second-largest military quarters of the dictator Fulgencio Batista. Bullet holes serve as a reminder of Fidel Castro's failed coup of 26 July 1953. Today, the building houses a school and a *Revolution Museum (Ctra. Central/corner Gen. Portuondo | Tue–Sat 9am–7pm, Sun 9am–12.30pm, admission 2 CUC)*.

MUSEO PROVINCIAL EMILIO BACARDÍ

Adorned by columns, this temple of archaeology and city history was founded in 1899 as the first museum on Cuba. The writing desk of founder Emilio Bacardí Moreau stands at the entrance. *C/ Pío Rosado/Aguilera | Mon–Fri 9am–5pm, Sat 9am–7pm, Sun 9am–3pm | admission 2 CUC*

GODS, CULTS & SAINTS

Have you ever met a Cuban dressed from head to toe in white? Including his shoes, socks and neck scarf? In Cuba, the phrase "to make the saint" *(hacerse santo)* is used to describe the initiation ceremony to become a *babalawo* (a practitioner of the Afro-Cuban religion of Santería) where white has to be worn after their indoctrination in the rituals, songs and stories of the Santería. It is the most widely spread religion on Cuba. This natural religion starts from the premise that every human being has been allocated at least one deity, Ochún, for instance, the goddess of vanity, Oyá, the dangerous goddess of vengeance, Yemayá, goddess of the sea and maternity, or Ogún, the womanizer, warrior and god of the mountains. Would you like to know which God best suits you? Simply ask a babalawo!

FOOD & DRINK

1900

The setting rather than the cuisine is what attracts guests to this state-owned peso restaurant housed in the former residence of the Barcardí family. The *sopa de mariscos* (seafood soup) is particularly good. *Daily noon –midnight | C/ San Basilio | betw. San Félix/Carnicería | tel. 22 62 35 07 | Budget*

PALADAR SALÓN TROPICAL

One of the very first paladars and still as good as ever. Here you'll be served Cuban, Italian, and grilled delicacies cooked by expert hands and served on a lovely roof terrace. *Daily 1pm–midnight | C/ Fernández Marcané 310 | Santa Bárbara | tel. 22 64 11 61 | Budget*

INSIDER TIP ST. PAULI

Yes, the name of this restaurant is linked to the cult German football club from Hamburg. After living in Germany for some time, this Cuban fan thought it would be a good omen to name his unusual restaurant after the club. Creative dishes at an excellent value for money. *Daily | Enramada 605/betw. Barnada/ Plaza de Marte | tel. 22 65 22 92 | Budget–Moderate*

ZÚNZUN

Feast in style either in the rooms or on the terrace of a villa. Large selection of tasty dishes, including Cuban specialities and seafood. *Daily noon–11pm | Av. Manduley 159/C/ 7 | Vista Alegre | tel. 22 64 01 75 | Budget–Expensive*

SHOPPING

CASA DEL HABANO

Large selection of cigars for lovers of world-class smokes. The shop belongs to the local tobacco factory. *Av. Jesús Menéndez 703 | daily 9am–6pm | admission ticket for visit (5 CUC) from Cubatur at the cathedral*

LIBRERÍA LA ESCALERA

Treasure chest for antique books, newspapers, posters and cards – a cult bookshop. *C/ Heredia 265 | daily 10am–10pm*

TIENDA DE LA MÚSICA

The wide spectrum of Cuban music, including bolero, son or cubaton. *C/ José A. Saco 306 | Mon–Sat 9am–5pm*

ENTERTAINMENT

CABARET TROPICANA

Held outdoors every Friday (10pm), Santiago's magnificent cabaret show is full of sensuality and emotion. *Circunvalación/Autopista Nacional, km 1.5 | tel. 22 64 25 79 | admission 30 CUC*

CASA DE LAS TRADICIONES

Smoke-filled dance bar full of Santería flair in the slightly disreputable red-light district. Walls are decorated with photos of Tivoli stars and orishas (Santería Gods). Occasional live music performances, INSIDER TIP Ogún ceremony on July 6. *C/ Rabi 154 | Tivoli | daily from 9pm*

CASA DE LA TROVA ★ ●

Small stage, walls adorned with photos, a few intimate seats for friends: talented singers and musicians perform here. The attractively furnished old room leads to the evening dancefloor *Patio de la Trova;* above you can dance until the early hours at the *Salon de los Grands. C/ Heredia 208 | daily 9pm–1am | admission 5 CUC*

MATAMOROS

This cosy bar plays homage to the fifties group *Trio Matamoros* with walls full of pictures and live bolero and son music. *Daily from 8pm | Plaza de Dolores*

PATIO ARTEX SANDUNGA
Ideal for winding down after your stroll through the city: Live music, nice patio, drinks, snacks and souvenirs. *C/ Heredia 304 | daily 5pm–1am | admission free*

WHERE TO STAY

CASA EL TIVOLI
The proprietor Sr. Luis Antonio Félix ("Luisito") and his wife Denia were made famous by the German writer Matthias Politycki who spent a year in this establishment and wrote about this couple in his novel. *C/ Jesús Rabi 107.5 | betw. Princesa and Santa Rosa | tel. 22 65 28 31 | lantoniofr@gmail.com | Budget*

CASA GRANDA
From the terrace of this splendidly restored former grand hotel (1914) you have a view across the entire *Parque Céspedes. 58 rooms, 3 suites | Parque Céspedes | tel. 22 65 30 21 | www.ho telescubanacan.com | Moderate*

DOÑA MARÍA ELENA PONCE FAVERO
Private residence furnished with fabulous antiques. The hospitable hosts rent out 2 private rooms (both with bathroom, air-conditioning and fridge). *C/ Hartmann 213 | betw. Maceo/San Mateo | tel. 22 65 12 97 | Budget*

E IMPERIAL
A famous landmark in Santiago. This magnificent, four-floor hotel is adorned with arched windows and balustrades. Great view from the ☼ rooftop garden. *39 rooms | C/ Enramadas/Santo Tomás | tel. 22 68 71 71 | 22 68 71 62 | www.hotel escubanacan.com | Moderate*

E SAN BASILIO
This elegant old villa with eight large rooms enjoys a central location. *C/ San Basilio 403 | betw. C/ Calvario/Carnicería | tel. 22 65 17 02 | 22 65 16 87 | www. hotelescubanacan.com | Moderate*

Expect to hear the finest Cuban sounds in the Casa de la Trova

MELIÁ SANTIAGO DE CUBA

The hotel in the city. Tennis courts, gym and a Jacuzzi. The disco *Café Santiago (Sat from 11pm)* is the no. 1 in town. *302 rooms | Av. Las Américas/ C/ M | tel. 22 68 70 70 | www.meliacuba.com | Expensive*

Impressive eye-catcher in the mountains: the basilica of El Cobre

CUBATUR/INFOTUR

Tickets (tobacco factory), daytrips. *Parque Céspedes (opposite Casa Granda) | tel. 22 68 60 33 | daily noon–4.30pm*

WHERE TO GO

BAYAMO (134 B4) (*ℳ M6*)

Friendly people, attractive boulevard, relaxed atmosphere – people rave about the capital of the province Granma, Bayamo (pop. 160,000). This authentically Cuban city (founded in 1513) along the Río Cauto and close to the Sierry Maestra is surprisingly not awash with tourists. Or maybe it is the appeal of the city's most famous son, Carlos Manuel Céspedes (1819–1874) who issued the first decla-

ration of independence. His birthplace, today the *Museo Casa Natal del Padre de la Patria (C/ Maceo 57 | Tue–Fri 9am–5pm, Sat 9am–2pm /8–10pm, Sun 10am–1.30pm | admission 1 CUC)*, stands on the central Plaza de la Revolución. If you want to know what the "father of the nation" looked like, visit the ● **INSIDER TIP** *Museo de Cera (C/ General García 221 | betw. Masó/Lora | Tue–Fri 9am–5pm, Sat 10am–1pm, 7–10pm, Sun 9am–noon | admission 2 CUC)*, a small waxworks in the pedestrian zone *(Bulevar)*. A centrally located, comfortable accomodation is the *Villa Léon (2 rooms | C/ Donato Marmol 154 | tel. (23) 41 12 88 | Budget)*.

EL COBRE (134 C5) (*ℳ N6*)

This small pilgrimage site, at the same time the centre of copper mining, lies a 20-minute drive from Santiago de Cuba in the mountains beyond Melgarejo. The white basilica (1927) crowning the green hill can be seen from afar. Inside the patron saint of Cuba, the *Virgen de la Caridad*, is enthroned above the altar. ● Sunflowers sold on the roadside are offerings to her heathen equivalent, the goddess Oshun. The car park has a view of the spoil heaps belonging to the copper mines.

LA COMANDANCIA DE LA PLATA ★ (134 B5) (*ℳ M6*)

A hike to the *Comandancia de La Plata* leads back to the beginnings of the revolution and into the national park surrounding Cuba's highest peak, *Pico Turquino* (1,974 m/6,476 ft) in the Sierra Maestra. The best starting point for the five-hour hike *(20 CUC incl. guide)* is the mountain village of *Santo Domingo* (73 km/45 miles southwest of Bayamo). In order to start off early in the morning, you're best off spending the night before at the ◉ *Villa Santo Domingo* hotel *(20 rooms | Ctra. La Plata, km 16 |*

tel. (23) 56 55 68 | Budget–Moderate). The Comandancia de Ejército Rebelde of La Plata served as a hiding place for the revolutionaries around Fidel Castro after their landing from Mexico to prepare the revolution. The first thing you see is the clearing where Castro landed in 1976 by helicopter. Then you can discover 16 buildings scattered on the estate, amongst them the field hospital where Che looked after the injured, Fidel Castro's Casa Comandante and the "Palace of Justice". A model in the museum shows the whole extent of the compound at a glance.

PARQUE DE BACONAO
(135 D5) (*M* O6)

Declared a biosphere reserve by Unesco, this 800 km²/309 sq mile park is Cuba's largest recreation area. A snake path leads you up the Gran Piedra, the region's highest mountain standing 1,234 m/4,049 ft high. On your way to the ✲ Mirador (viewing platform), the Museo Cafetal La Isabelica (daily 8am–4pm | admission 2 CUC) is worth a stop; this former coffee finca was founded in 1791 by migrants from the former Sainte-Domingue (renamed Haiti in 1804). On the coast again, along the Ctra. Bacanao (km 9.5), there's the "Prehistoric Valley" (see p. 111) with reproductions of dinosaurs and other prehistoric creatures. Under a mile further on, car lovers will appreciate the Museo Nacional del Transporte Terrestre (Ctra. Baconao, km 8.5 | daily 8am–5pm | admission 1 CUC): the 44 vintage cars include the Ford driven by Fidel Castro's mother Lina Ruz. A small building shows 2,500 miniature model cars. At the kilometre 27.5 mark on Ctra. Bacanao, the Acuario Baconao (Tue–Sat 9am–5pm | admission from 7 CUC) draws visitors with a delfinarium, which unfortunately isn't species-appropriate. On the Ctra. Baconao then appears the double hotel Club Amigo Carisol Los Corales (310 rooms | tel. 22 35 61 15 | Budget | day guests pay 20 CUC) on a beautiful sandy beach – this is one of the Cubans' favourite destinations just as the Laguna Baconao at the end of the Ctra. Baconao.

PILÓN/MAREA DEL PORTILLO/ PARQUE NACIONAL GRANMA
(133 E6) (*M* L6)

The coastal road west of Santiago de Cuba is amongst the most beautiful stretches in Cuba; it is, however, in a bad state. Continually hugging a dramatic coast lined by bays, it leads to Chivirico at km 60 (holiday resort Brisas Sierra Mar Hotel, also for day visitors), then drive past the foot of the Pico Turquino to the Villa Turística Punta Piedra (13 rooms | tel. (23) 59 70 62 | Budget) in Marea del Portillo until your reach the small town of Pilón. West of Pilón marks the start of the Parque Nacional Desembarco del Granma (national park honouring the landing of the Granma). For its high number of endemic plants and animals, the park was included on the World Heritage list in 1999. It extends to the Playa Las Coloradas, where in 1956 Fidel Castro and his men arrived on the Granma from exile in Mexico.

LOW BUDGET

The Plaza de Marte in Santiago is full of activity on Sundays, especially for children: snack stands, fairground booths, animals and small carousels.

Every Sunday (10am–11am), visiting the Casa de Velázquez in Santiago is worth your while twice over, as Peña de Danzón performances are included in the admission price.

DISCOVERY TOURS

① CUBA AT A GLANCE

START: ① Havana **END:** ① Havana	**12 days** Driving time (without stops) approx. 40 hours
Distance: 🚗 2,525 km/1,569 miles	

COSTS: around 2,700 CUC for 2 people for hire car, entry to the national park with guide, accommodation in basic hotels or *casas particulares*, food, snacks, petrol

WHAT TO PACK: swimwear, sun protection, hiking boots, binoculars, rain gear, basics for your journey, Cuban Pesos for shopping in the provinces

IMPORTANT TIPS: Do not forget your passport (or a copy) for the journey to and from both causeways *(pedrapléns).*
Hiking to the ⑬ Comandancia de la Plata takes approx. 5 hrs

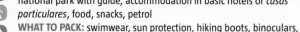

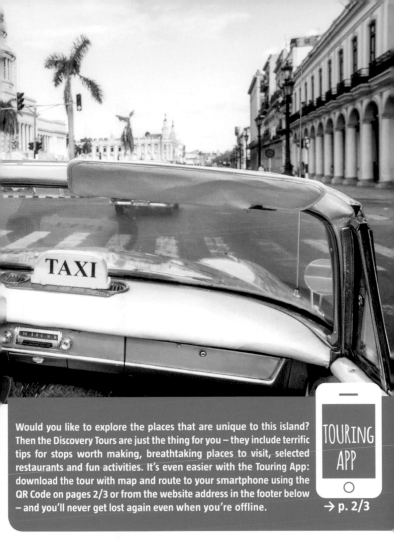

Would you like to explore the places that are unique to this island? Then the Discovery Tours are just the thing for you – they include terrific tips for stops worth making, breathtaking places to visit, selected restaurants and fun activities. It's even easier with the Touring App: download the tour with map and route to your smartphone using the QR Code on pages 2/3 or from the website address in the footer below – and you'll never get lost again even when you're offline.

TOURING APP

→ p. 2/3

Can you explore the largest island in the Caribbean in just two weeks? Of course you can! Take this route from the island's capital Havanna to the idyllic beaches on the northern coast, follow the traces of the revolution to the east and discover the sugar cane towns in the south.

Leave **① Havana → p. 32 via the tunnel and then fol-low the Vía Blanca;** this road takes you through Cojímar → p. 48 and Playas del Este → p. 48 until, at the **② Puente Bacunayagua,** you reach the viewpoint **Mira-dor del Yumurí** (in front of the bridge), which invites you to

DAY 1
① Havana
85 km/53 mi
② Puente Bacunayagua

Photo: Taxi driver passing the Capitol in Havana

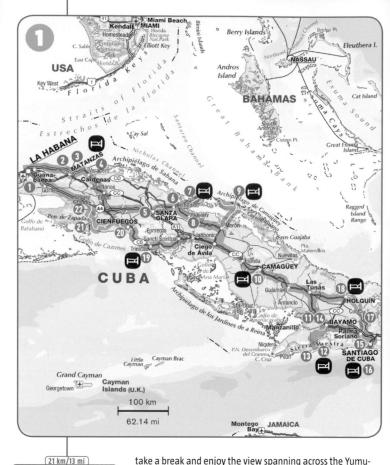

| 21 km/13 mi |
| ❸ Matanzas 🍽️ |

| 40 km/25 mi |
| ❹ Varadero |
| ♿ 🏖️ 🍴 🍸 🛏️ |

take a break and enjoy the view spanning across the Yumurí valley. When you enter ❸ **Matanzas → p. 61** you'll be treated to fantastic scenery of the vast bay and, when you leave, of the Río Canimar valley. The road then takes you on to Cuba's oldest tourist resort ❹ **Varadero → p. 56**, with its famous beach, restaurants, bars and hotels. The **Cubatur → p. 60** tourist information centre can provide you with a list of hotels in Varadero as well as on Cayo Las Brujas and Cayo Guillermo (route points 7 and 9) if you haven't already booked your accommodation in advance.

DAY 2–3

The humble reality of Cuban life can be witnessed in nearby Cardenas → p. 60 where horse-drawn carriages are still used to get around. **Drive through the town, always straight ahead, in the direction of Máximo Gómez;** sugarcane fields and tropical fruit plantations now dominate the scenery past Colón to ⑤ **Santa Clara → p. 70,** where fans from around the world gather at the **Museo Memorial del Ernesto Che Guevara.** Now it's back to colonial times in the old town of ⑥ **Remedios → p. 71;** where its old buildings remind you of the country's former glory days, such as the **La Casona Cueto,** once a colonial palace and now a hotel. It's worth carrying on to the coast to spend the night there **so drive across the causeway to ⑦ Cayo Las Brujas → p. 71,** and check in for two nights at the **Villa Las Brujas.**

Then discover the less-known route along the coast from Caribarien to ⑧ **Yaguajay,** and visit the **Museo Nacional Camilo Cienfuegos** *(Mon–Sat 8am–4pm, Sun 9am–1pm | admission 1 CUC)* where you'll find the monument of the revolutionary Camilo Cienfuegos who disappeared under mysterious circumstances. Then head to **Morón → p. 70,** the gateway to the ⑨ **Jardines del Rey → p. 68,** which is reached by crossing another causeway. Enjoy a one-day (two nights) holiday on **Cayo Guillermo** in the beach hotel **Sercotel Club Cayo Guillermo** *(en.clubcayoguillermo.com | Expensive)* – with splendid diving and swimming opportunities at the picturesque **Playa Pilar.**

You now turn your back on the coast and head to the heart of the island at ⑩ **Camagüey → p. 63** where you can find accommodation for the night in the town's old streets. Visit the pretty colonial **Plaza San Juan de Dios** and take a look at the paintings in the **Jover** gallery and count the number of church steeples in the city from the viewpoint of the **Antiguo Hospital de Dios.**

Now return to the Carretera Central and head in the direction of Las Tunas following a signposted road on your right along the vast Río Cauto plain to ⑪ Bayamo → p. 86. It's worth exploring this untouristy Cuban town and take a stroll past the shops and restaurants on the main Calle General García. **Head off again before dark driving past Bartolomé Masó to ⑫ Santo Domingo.** Check in to the hotel **Villa Santo Domingo → p. 86** where you can also organise a local guide (20 CUC, 5 CUC camera) who can take you on a hike to the Comandancia de la Plata the next day.

212 km/132 mi

⑤ Santa Clara

49 km/30 mi

⑥ Remedios

53 km/33 mi

⑦ Cayo Las Brujas

DAY 4–5

71 km/44 mi

⑧ Yaguajay

137 km/85 mi

⑨ Jardines del Rey

DAY 6

265 km/165 mi

⑩ Camagüey

DAY 7

204 km/127 mi

⑪ Bayamo

66 km/41 mi

⑫ Santo Domingo

How the sugar barons lived: Palacio del Valle in Cienfuegos

DAY 8

7 km/4.3 mi

🕭 Comandancia de la Plata 🏛 🌳

72 km/45 mi

🕮 Bayamo 🍴

108 km/67 mi

🕯 El Cobre 🏠

If you set off early, you'll be able to catch sights and sounds of the birds and small animals in the park. Most tours start up at 7am and breakfast is served early in the hotel. **First drive through the barrier of the national park (right next to the hotel) and make your way up Cuba's steepest road (almost a 45° ascent) to reach the actual starting point of the hike after 5 km/3.1 miles at Alto de Naranjo.** If you're not keen on driving up the road yourself, you'll always find friendly Cubans at the barrier who will offer to take you up. **For an hour, the hiking trail takes you along a stony and, in parts, slippery path** to the house of Oswaldo Medina (which you'll reach after about an hour) – this is good practice for the second more adventurous and steeper section of the route up to the **🕭 Comandancia de la Plata → p. 86** (sturdy boots are required for this stage!). The path around the former rebel's hideout is a relaxed stroll in comparison. The excursion ends around 1–2pm.

Now continue from Santo Domingo and take a break for refreshment in nearby 🕮 Bayamo, for example in the restaurant **San Salvador** (daily noon–11pm | C/ A. Maceo 107/ betw. Martí/Marmol | tel. (23) 42 69 41 | Budget–Moderate) and head to **🕯 El Cobre → p. 86** past **Contramaestre and Palma Soriano. H**ere you can visit the church dedicated to the patron saint of Cuba, Virgen de la Caridad. The "swinging" city of ⑯ **Santiago de Cuba** → p. 81 is now close by and is signposted from this point. You're best checking into the **Meliá Santiago de Cuba** → p. 86 or, on the opposite side of the road, the more basic option **Isla-zul Las Americas** *(70 rooms | Av. de Las Américas y General Cebreco | tel. 22 64 20 11 | www.islazul.cu | Moderate)*; both hotels offer safe parking spaces and are close to the Auto-pista 1. Be sure to spend an evening in the **Casa de la Tro-va** → p. 84 while staying in Cuba's music capital to hear the finest Cuban sounds.

Make sure you've seen the balcony where Fidel Castro an-nounced the victory in the Cuban Revolution at the Parque Céspedes before leaving Santiago. Now follow the traces of the Castro brothers further inland. **Take the Autopista 1 out of Santiago and turn off right to Julio A. Mella. Shortly be-fore reaching Loinaz Hechevarría, take the mountain road leading up to ⑰ Birán** → p. 79. The old family residence of the Castro brothers, the **Finca Mañacas**, is located at the edge of the village. **Once you have visited the estate, head back to the road and drive on to Loinaz Hechevarría and then continue past Barajagua to ⑱ Holguín** → p. 78, the tourist hotspot on Cuba's eastern side. You can enjoy the best views of the province's capital from your hotel **Mira-dor de Mayabe**. Treat yourself to an evening meal at the restaurant **1910** *(C/ Mártires 143/betw. Aricocha/Cables | tel. 24 42 39 94 | Moderate)*.

On the next morning, set off on the long drive back west-wards to the romantic Unesco World Heritage town of Trinidad with the sugar-cane valley **Valle de los Ingenios** → p. 72 and its bell tower. The fairy-tale resort oft ⑲ **Trin-idad** → p. 72 has been lovingly preserved and is home to a new gastronomic scene. Enjoy a stroll around its streets and a dance on the large flight of steps leading up to the **Casa de Música**! Spend two nights to recover from the long journey in one of the many private bed and breakfasts *(ca-sas particulares)*.

The next station is ⑳ **Cienfuegos** → p. 66 on the Pun-ta Gorda peninsula. In between the rows of elegant villas stands the **Palacio de Valle,** Cuba's most pompous pal-ace built for a sugar baron. You could now quickly head back to Havanna on the autopista, **but you turn left from the Circuito Sur before Guayabales to Yaguaramas and**

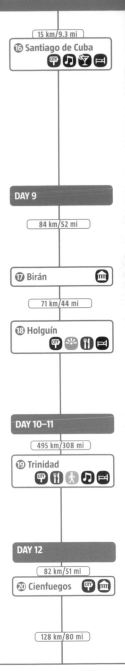

15 km/9.3 mi
⑯ Santiago de Cuba

DAY 9

84 km/52 mi

⑰ Birán

71 km/44 mi

⑱ Holguín

DAY 10–11

495 km/308 mi

⑲ Trinidad

DAY 12

82 km/51 mi

⑳ Cienfuegos

128 km/80 mi

㉑ Bahía de Cochinas

87 km / 54 mi

㉒ La Boca

168 km / 104 mi

❶ Havana

from there onwards to Playa Girón. This route offers a nice glimpse ino country life and leads to the **㉑ Bahía de Cochinas (bay of pigs)** → p. 61, famous for the military invasion in 1961. The **Museo de la Intervención** documents this failed operation. **40 km/25 miles further north along the swamp region Ciénaga de Zapata** → p. 61 to **㉒ La Boca**, where you can take a boat ride over the **Laguna del Tesoro** and visit a **crocodile breeding station.** From this point it's just 18 km/11 miles to the A1 and another 150 km/93 miles back to **❶ Havana**.

❷ THE GREEN WEST: ORCHIDS, CORK OAKS AND LIME MOUNTAINS

START: ❶ Havana END: ❶ Havana	5 days Driving time (without stops) 8 hours
Distance: 🚗 430 km/269 miles	

COSTS: around 475 CUC for the guide, petrol, admission costs, accommodation for two people, food, parking fees in Palma Rubia, ferry to Cayo Levisa plus around 375 CUC for the hire car

WHAT TO PACK: hiking boots, picnic, rain gear, sun protection, water, copy of passport, Cuban Pesos for buying fruit and snacks in the countryside

IMPORTANT TIPS: Arrive in Palma Rubia by 9.30am for the ferry to ❼ Cayo Levisa. Poor conditions on the road from Palma Rubia to Mariel! The hike around the ❻ Valle de Viñales takes around 3 hours on foot

The oldest part of Cuba offers amazing scenery, one particular highlight being the Valle de Viñales with its mystic limestone mountains. Along this route discover the ecological oasis on Cuba and the paradise island of Cayo Levisa on the way back.

DAY 1

❶ Havana

79 km / 49 mi

Leave **❶ Havana** → p. 32 by taking Avenida 5 (Miramar), then Calle 146 (left turn-off to the Centro de las Convenciones) and then Avenidas 25 and 23 as the most direct way to reach the motorway *(autopista)* to Pinar del Río. After around 60 km, follow the wooden signpost directing you right to "Las Terrazas". After a short distance uphill, you reach the information centre (providing a good map of the region) where you have to pay 2 CUC admission fee to enter the *Puerta de las Delicias* and continue to

the ecotourism complex **❷ Las Terrazas → p. 53**, beautifully located in a wide valley with a lake. The brave-hearted can try their hand climbing along an INSIDER TIP 1.6 km/1 mile long canopy tour(from 25 CUC) near the **Hotel Moka**, where you spend your first night.

Just a few kilometres further on is the green rural resort of **❸ Soroa → p. 53** with its famous orchid garden; **the road takes you straight back to the motorway and on to Pinar del Río.** It is worth taking a small detour to the mountain resort of **❹ San Diego de los Baños → p. 53**, with its thermal spa (straight opposite Hotel **Mirador**)with water heated to 30–40°. The roots of Cuba's tourism lie here. Now return to the motorway and drive all the way to the busy provincial capital **❺ Pinar del Río → p. 51**, with banks and Internet cafés. Take a look at the lovingly presented natural history collection at the **Museo de Ciencias Naturales** in the Palacio Guash. The best private restaurant, the **Paladar El Mesón → p. 52**, is situated straight opposite the museum.

From Pinar del Río it's just 30 km (19 miles) to the ❻ Valle de Viñales → p. 54, where you will spend the next two nights. The best way to explore the amazing geographical landscape around the limestone mountains known as

❷ Las Terrazas

DAY 2–3

18 km/11 mi

❸ Soroa

52 km/33 mi

❹ San Diego de los Baños

53 km/33 mi

❺ Pinar del Río

25 km/16 mi

❻ Valle de Viñales

mogotes is on foot or by horse. You can arrange a guide (3 hours: 10 CUC) at the **Centro de Visitantes** when you enter the Valle de Viñales or at the **Museo Municipal** in Viñales *(Mon–Sat 8am–10pm, Sun 8am–4pm | Salvador Cisneros 115 | tel. 48 79 33 95).* If you choose to stay at the **Casa Tito Crespo** *(3 rooms | Las Maravillas 58 | tel. 48 79 33 83 | nauryc@princesa.pri.sld.cu | Budget)* situated on the road to Puerto Esperanza, you will have your own tour guide in house: The owner's son Diosnel Crespo is a qualified guide and explores the less well-known routes sometimes even on horseback. The guides set off on the three-hour excursions at 7am in the morning with the mist rising from the mogotes, the air still fresh and the blossoms on the *Varita de San José* still white (they turn pink in the evening light). Accompanied by the fast rising sun over the mountains, the red soil trail takes you past tobacco fields to the modest farmhouses of the tobacco growers and along narrow paths at the foot of the towering limestone mountains. You learn a lot about the traditional crops grown here such as corn (often grown together with beans), sweet potatoes or pineapple, about tropical plants and trees such as the calabash tree or sandbox tree and native flora such as the *Ceibón de la Sierra de los Òrganos.* The famous endemic cork oak has become so rare that it can only be seen in the museum (see above).

The Valle de Viñales is an area ideal for hiking

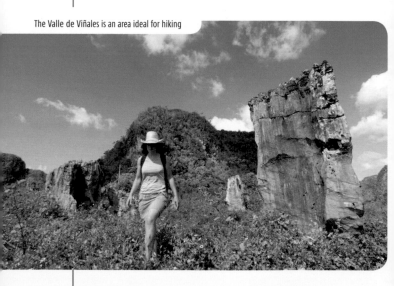

You can find these tours as an app at: go.marco-polo.com/cub

If you want to spend a day at the beach to end your tour in style, then book a night at the **Villa Cayo Levisa** with **Infotur** *(daily 8am–8pm | C/ Salvador Cisneros 63 B | tel. 48 79 62 63 | www.infotur.cu)* or at a hotel agency. **Then head off at 8am at the latest on the next day to arrive on time at the ferry port in Palma Rubia by 9.30am.** The island **7 Cayo Levisa → p. 55** also offers an amazing beach and a fantastic spot for diving. After a relaxing final day, return to **1 Havana on the Carretera Panamericana via Bahía Honda and the new container port Mariel (Boca).**

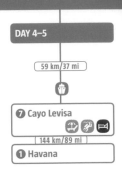

DAY 4–5

59 km/37 mi

7 Cayo Levisa

144 km/89 mi

1 Havana

---

③ TO THE CAYOS AND PLAYAS ON THE NORTHERN COAST

START: **1** Playa Santa Lucía End: **1** Playa Santa Lucía	**4 days** Driving time (without stops) **12 hours**
Distance: ⏱ **675 km/419 miles**	

COSTS: around 375 CUC for petrol, accommodation, food and journey to the *pedraplén* plus approx. 310 CUC for the hire car
WHAT TO PACK: binoculars, swimwear, sun protection, drinking water, Cuban Pesos for buying fruit and snacks at stands and bars in the provinces

IMPORTANT TIPS: do not forget your passport (or a copy) and 4 CUC to cross the causeway.

This route is ideal for those looking for an adventure and would like to take a closer look at the neighbouring holiday paradise too. If you are based at Playa Santa Lucía, visit Cayo Coco and Cayo Guillermo or vice versa. You will have chance to explore Camagüey on your way back.

If you are based in Playa Santa Lucía → p. 66 then reserve a room for the next two nights in the **Aparthotel Azul → p. 69**, so you don't end up without accommodation at your destination. If you're taking the tour in the opposite direction – if you're based on Cayo Coco → p. 68 – the best is to book a room at the *casa particular* **INSIDER TIP** **Casa Mar Verde** *(2 rooms | at the town entrance | tel. 0 54 04 41 44 | Budget)* and follow the directions below in the opposite direction.

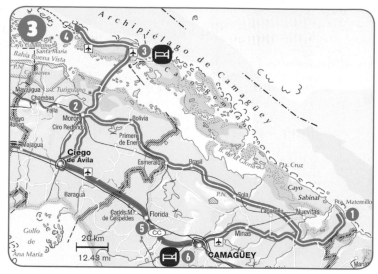

DAY 1–2

① Playa Santa Lucía

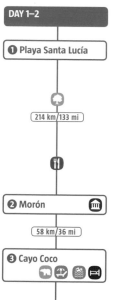

214 km/133 mi

② Morón 🏛

58 km/36 mi

③ Cayo Coco
🐾 🔄 🏖 🛏

The route takes you from **① Playa Santa Lucía** leading southwards to Camagüey, **but after approx. 44 km (27 miles) after passing the crossroads to Camalote, take a sharp right to San Miguel de Bagá and Nuevitas. At the next *punto de control* (40 km/24 miles an hour) continue straight on** along the quiet coastal road past Sola and Esmeralda to Morón. The only sights along this road are cows, sugar cane and banana groves and the railway crossings remind you of the region's sugar cane past. Rice grown inland is also left out to dry here under the vast Caribbean skies. Shortly before reaching Morón, take a break in the rustic **Parador Batán** *(open 24 hours, payment in Cuban Pesos only)*.

② Morón → p. 70 is a pretty rural town with an old railway station worth visiting. After another stretch of about 20 minutes, you've quickly reached the barrier for the *pedraplén*, the 17 km (11 mile)-long causeway leading to **③ Cayo Coco → p. 68. Here you have to provide documentary proof (passport) that you are a tourist and pay a 2 CUC toll per person (the same applies on the way back).** During the drive across the causeway you will see flocks of pink flamingos flying past or stood in the water on both the left and right. At the information stand, prettily roofed with palm leaves, you can usually

Caribbean beach feeling on Cayo Guillermo

buy a map with the layout of the hotels on the island to make it easier to find the freely accessible beaches. The prettiest beach lies at the very end of **④ Cayo Guillermo**, which is also connected with Cayo Coco by a drivable causeway: the **Playa Pilar** with crystal-clear water, powdery white sand and the small island of **Media Luna** opposite. Spending the day in an XL comfort beach bed on the beach costs 10 CUC (3 Drinks included!), renting a simple deckchair 2 CUC. The restaurant serves drinks and snacks (including seafood).

After visiting this archipelago known as the **Jardines del Rey** → p. 68 do not take the same route back to Playa Santa Lucia but instead drive through Morón down to Ciego de Ávila and then take a left onto the Carretera Central. In the small town of **⑤ Florida** you can take a break for refreshment at the **Caney** café before you carry on to **⑥ Camagüey** → p. 63 where you need to be fully concentrated. **Follow the signposts to the old town and to the Plaza San Juan de Dios. Your accommodation for the night is just two streets away at Calle Lugareño 121 (on the corner between San Rafael and San Clemente): Casa Austria** → p. 65, which is recognisable with the flags flying in front of the entrance. Your friendly host Josef Leopold originally comes from Austria and

33 km / 21 mi

④ Cayo Guillermo

DAY 3

211 km / 131 mi

⑤ Florida

40 km / 25 mi

⑥ Camagüey

is a well-known personality in his adopted country: he is a lawyer and has represented in the past the local association of writers. He also runs a patisserie in **Café Sissi** and the patio restaurant next door (with its delicious goulash!) which both enrich the city's gastronomic scene.

DAY 4

117 km/73 mi

① Playa Santa Lucía

After visiting the city, return to ① **Playa Santa Lucía** by **leaving Camagüey in a north-easterly direction along Avenida Carlos J. Finlay.** At the half way point, you'll pass the **Parador Santa Isabel** (open 24 hours a day) with the remains of a sugar factory.

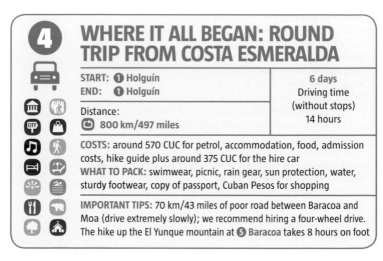

4 WHERE IT ALL BEGAN: ROUND TRIP FROM COSTA ESMERALDA

START: ① Holguín END: ① Holguín	6 days Driving time (without stops) 14 hours
Distance: 🚗 800 km/497 miles	

COSTS: around 570 CUC for petrol, accommodation, food, admission costs, hike guide plus around 375 CUC for the hire car
WHAT TO PACK: swimwear, picnic, rain gear, sun protection, water, sturdy footwear, copy of passport, Cuban Pesos for shopping

IMPORTANT TIPS: 70 km/43 miles of poor road between Baracoa and Moa (drive extremely slowly); we recommend hiring a four-wheel drive. The hike up the El Yunque mountain at ⑤ **Baracoa** takes 8 hours on foot

This route takes you in the footsteps of Fidel Castro, the conqueror Velázquez and Taíno to explore Cuba's east. You will encounter two obstacles along the way: the journey along the traitorous yet extremely scenic coastal road and the hike up the El Yunque.

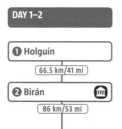

DAY 1–2

① Holguín

66.5 km/41 mi

② Birán

86 km/53 mi

As you are probably staying in one of the holiday resorts on Costa Esmeralda, start your tour in the neighbouring city of ① **Holguín** → p. 78. **Follow the Carretera de Mayarí (123) from Holguín to Barajagua where you turn off right to Loynaz Hecheverría. Pass through the town and follow the signposted direction up to ② Birán** → p. 79. You'll spot the entrance to the estate where Fidel and Raúl Castro grew up, **Finca Mañacas,** upon leaving Birán again. **Stop to visit the finca and then head to Mella via Julio Antonio Mella where the A1 takes you to ③ San-**

DISCOVERY TOURS

tiago de Cuba → p. 81 **in about an hour.** This is where Fidel Castro went to school and you can see old photos of him hanging in the corridor right behind the entrance of the former **Jesuit college** (*daily 8am–8pm | donation 1 CUC*), located to the right of the Dolores church on the Plaza de Dolores. While at the school, Castro lived with a family from Haiti in house no. 6 on the Calle General Jesús Rabí in the French immigrant district of Tivoli. On your way to this legendary road, you'll walk past the central park **Parque Céspedes**. The city hall is where Fidel Castro once proclaimed the victory of the revolution from its blue balcony on the evening of January 1st, 1959. Diagonally opposite the city hall, the Moorish ventilation grilles on the **Casa de Velázquez** → p. 82, (Cuba's oldest house) are reminiscent of Cuba's colonial past. The conqueror and first governor of Cuba, Diego Velázquez de Cuéllar, died here in 1524. In order to visit **Fidel Castro's grave** on the Cementerio Santa Ifigenia (*Av. Crombet | daily 8am–6pm | admission 1 CUC, photo permit 1 CUC*) and also be able to dance a little in the famous music pub **Casa de la Trova,** you should definitely stay in Santiago for two nights.

Leave Santiago de Cuba the next morning on the A1, turn off after a few miles to the country road towards El

❸ Santiago de Cuba

DAY 3–4

120 km / 75 mi

④ Mirador La Gobernadora 🌳 🍴

119 km / 74 mi

⑤ Baracoa 🏛 🕴 🛍 🏃 🌳 🚐

DAY 5

202 km / 126 mi

Cristo, Alto Songo and La Maya and reach the motorway leading to Guantánamo, which you then bypass by following the signs to Baracoa. Soon you'll pass a closed barrier on your right. It used to lead to the Mirador de los Malones, a viewpoint for the Bahía de Guantánamo. But there's a new one now: the **④ Mirador La Gobernadora → p. 77** a further 5–10 minutes by car on a hill. From there you can look at the bay through binoculars and have something to eat. Following that, enjoy the drive along the Caribbean coast **until you reach the road on your left to Baracoa along the bendy pass road Farola through the mountains.** The regional speciality of *cucurucho* is often sold along the road: a sweet delicacy made from coconut, guava, pineapple, orange and sugar wrapped in palm leaves. The Farola road ends at **⑤ Baracoa → p. 75**, a pretty town at the foot of the towering El Yunque mountain (575 m/1837 ft). When Diego de Velázquez landed here and founded the city in 1511, the distinctive mountain was still an Indian place of worship. The four-hour climb to the top is well worth it as you are treated to an amazing sight; however it should only be attempted accompanied by a guide as the path through rain forest scenery is extremely steep in parts. **Infotur** *(C/ Maceo 129 | Mon–Sat 8.30am–4.45pm | tel. (21) 64 17 81 | www.cubatravel.cu)* offers organised tours. If the hike is too strenuous for you, explore instead the friendly atmosphere of Cuba's oldest city, take a look at the old portrait photos of native Indians in the small **Museo Municipal** at the **Fortaleza Matachín**, visit the limestone cave **Cueva del Paraíso** and the **Casa del Cacao**, where you can taste excellent chocolate made in the region. A chocolate factory founded by Che Guevara in 1963 is still situated at the edge of Baracoa on the road to Moa. If you want to spend the night close to the beach, drive to hotel **Villa Maguana** at kilometre 22 for an idyllic setting with its own private beach.

The drive to Moa is one of Cuba's most scenic routes if not one of the toughest. **Parts of it are on dirt road so you can only drive very slowly paying full attention;** stunning views of the bays, river estuaries and mountains as well as small breaks for example at the entrance to the **Humboldt National Park → p. 77**, do their best to compensate for this difficult drive. **Shortly before reaching Moa, the road is good again and you continue along the coast until you reach the turn-off to**

The Humboldt National Park protects a large section of the Caribbean rain forest

⑥ Cayo Saetía → p. 79. Here you can spend the night in **Hotel Villa Cayo Saetía** so that you have enough time to enjoy the pretty beach, a dip in the sea and maybe even a INSIDER TIP safari to the ostriches and antelopes living on the island.

Now close to the end of your round trip, you'll encounter traces of Fidel Castro again. As the son of the wealthy farmer and land owner Ángel Castro Argiz from Birán, he married the mayor's daughter (who gave birth to his first son Fidelito in 1949) in the church at **⑦ Banes → p. 78** Fulgencio Batista, who would go on to become the country's dictator and who also came from Banes, congratulated the couple by offering a gift. The marriage ended in 1955 when Castro became one of Batista's harshest critics. In the nearby **Museo Indocubano Baní** you can learn about the region's archaeological significance and admire a tiny golden Taíno statuette. From here it's not far to the **Museo Chorro de Maíta**, where you can view remains of supposedly the island's largest Indian cemetery. Opposite is the reconstructed Indian village of **Aldea Taína**. Both are situated on the road to Guardalavaca, the origins of Costa Esmeralda. **Well-paved roads take you back to ❶ Holguín.**

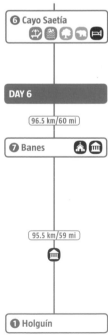

⑥ Cayo Saetía

DAY 6

96.5 km/60 mi

⑦ Banes

95.5 km/59 mi

❶ Holguín

SPORTS & ACTIVITIES

The sporting activities on offer are second to none on this Caribbean island, the most popular being walking, cycling, surfing and last but not least diving.

Yet Cuba also keeps up with the latest outdoor trends such as kitesurfing with its hotspot at Cayo Guillermo, or climbing in the valley of Viñales. And those with a head for heights can swing from tree to tree along zip lines stretching over the unspoilt valleys of Viñales and Las Terrazas. Tennis players have plenty of courts to choose from at the hotels. Adventure-minded motorcyclists can take a hedonist's tour of the Caribbean island: *Poderosa Tours (www.lapoderosa-tours.co)* has specialised in unforgettable **INSIDER TIP** Harley Davidson tours. Cuba's main sporting attraction is its many fantastic diving destinations around the tiny offshore islands.

CLIMBING

There are hundreds of climbing routes to choose from in the *mogotes* of Viñales – climbing fans rave about the challenging karst stone, the overhangs and the vegetation. The *Cuba Climbing* guide (£ 19.65) provides excellent tips. More information at *www.cubaclimbing.com*.

CYCLING

What was once a necessity for transportation has long since evolved into a cult on the Caribbean island. Today, international tour operators offer a staggering num-

Fans of water sports and and other nature lovers can look forward to sheer paradise in beach resorts and mountains or between 1001 islands

ber of cycling holidays and tours around Cuba and first-class bikes are offered as part of the deal. A particularly favourite route is between Trinidad and Cienfuegos. By now, **INSIDER TIP** many private hosts have bikes for rent, too *(5–8 CUC/day)* – ask about it at your accomodation!

DANCING

If you want to learn how to dance Cuban son, cha-cha-cha or salsa, you can book classes back home with a specialised op-erator (see p. 121) or on the island, e. g. at the *abc academia baile en cuba* (see p. 58) in Varadero. Most of the holiday resorts also offer salsa classes.

DIVING

Cuba's *diving sites* around the island are in a class of their own. Look forward to intact underwater worlds and clean wa-ter with 40 m/130 ft of visibility. A diving session costs from 35 euros. This is an overview of the best spots:

Cayo Largo: caves and drop-offs with great corals. You'll find a diving school at Playa Sirena.

Hola Club Faro Luna/Cienfuegos: a highlight are the many underwater canyons in the immediate vicinity of the diving basis.

Guardalavaca/Playas Esmeralda/Pesquero: diving in depths of 5–40 m/15–130 ft near the Bahamas Channel. Everywhere you look: caves, grottoes and coral valleys.

Isla de la Juventud: the area with the most diving spots on Cuba (56) lies between 13 and 20 nautical miles from Hotel Colony.

★ *Jardines de la Reina*: Once Fidel Castro's favourite fishing spot, the region became the *Parque Nacional Jardines de la Reina* in 1996. Located off the island's southern coast, it is rated as one of 100 best diving areas in the world and covers around 250 tiny islands; the reef is 120 km/75 miles long offering visibility down to 50 m/165 ft and an amazing variety of fish and corals. Tour operators organise guided safaris on diving boats where guests sleep on a hotel ship.

Jardines del Rey: coral gardens with soft and hard coral, grottoes, caves, canyons, crevasses and wrecks, all in crystal-clear waters (visibility around 40 m/130 ft) with an unusual abundance of fish, including whale sharks.

Marea del Portillo: diving and snorkelling area with 16 spots, amongst them entire forests of the rare black coral.

María La Gorda: the diving sites close to the coast (between 15 and 30 minutes by boat) lie at the outside reef, which drops down to depths of 2,500m/8,000ft. Due to the weak currents these are good grounds for beginners too.

Playa Santa Lucía: high numbers of fish appear between November and May; however, outside those months the sea is calmer. One attraction is INSIDER TIP feeding the sharks (bull sharks).

Santiago de Cuba: over 23 diving spots with wonderful tunnels, steep rock walls and coral mountains.

A refreshing and fun adrenalin rush sailing a catamaran

Varadero: coral reefs, caves and wrecks – all in all 30 diving spots await you all around the beach peninsula and its large tourist hotels.

For a comprehensive programme of diving trips to Cuba, contact *Regal Dive (tel. 01353 65 99 99 | www.regal-diving.co.uk)*.

FISHING

Ernest Hemingway is attributed with popularising this "sport" on Cuba. He was the most passionate angler of the last century and loved to go fishing in the Straits of Florida on Cuba's northern shore, an area teeming with fish. The best seasons for amateur anglers are the months of May to December. Fishing excursions are available at all marinas. *www.gaviota-grupo.com*

GOLF

The 18-hole golf course (72 par) of Varadero *(Varadero Golf Club | Av. Las Américas | www.varaderogolfclub.com)* boasts a beautiful location in the east of the peninsula on the lagoon. Playing 18 holes costs 70 CUC. There is also *Diplo-Golf (Ctra. de Vento, km 8 | Capdevila | tel. 07 845 45 78 | green fee 20 CUC),* a 9-hole golf course laid out in 1920 by homesick British expatriates, which also accepts visiting players. It is also known as "El Golfito".

HIKING

Hike up to the summit of the Pico Turquino or explore the Humboldt National Park, and walk through the forests around Topes de Collantes or Las Terrazas... Even though many of the *senderos* (hiking trails) are signposted: don't walk on your own, but only with a group. In the national parks, you even have to be accompanied by a state-licensed guide (registration and booking through the local information centres or agencies). For more information, contact *Ecotur (cubanaturetravel.com)*.

SAILING

Marinas with moorings or opportunities to hire boats are available for instance in Havana, Varadero and Cienfuegos *(check www.nauticamarlin.com | www.gaviota-grupo.com).* Entering by sea the crew has to contact the harbour authorities even before reaching sovereign waters (twelve nautical miles). For this, you have to use either the HF channels (SSB) 2760 (National Coastal Network) and 2790 (Tourism Network) or the VHF channels 68 for the National Coastal Network and 16 for the Tourism Network. Helpful literature: *Cuba – A Cruising Guide.*

WELLBEING

It is not really surprising that, in the land of bearded revolutionaries, the health and wellness segment has been slow to take off! However the major all-inclusive hotels have caught up with the trend and provide spas and treatments which meet high international standards such as the *YHI Spa* in *Paradisus Río de Oro & Spa* (see p. 80) in Playa Esmeralda

WIND-AND KITESURFING

Windsurfers find good to excellent wind conditions at the beaches of Cayo Guillermo, Guardalavaca, Playa Santa Lucía and Varadero (on average 2–6 Beaufort). All-inclusive hotels with a sizeable sports programme offer introductory courses. Cayo Guillermo in front of Cuba's northern coast has evolved into a kitesurfing hotspot *(www.kite-cuba.com)*.

TRAVEL
WITH KIDS

Until recently, big signs on Cuba's street read: "200 million children will be sleeping on the streets tonight. None of them will be Cuban". A proud statement which – propaganda or no propaganda – makes one thing clear: no matter what their origin and skin colour, all children are looked after here. And that has not changed.

If you know Latin America a little, you'll know that Cuba is the subcontinent's most progressive country in this respect. Travelling with your family you'll encounter a seriousness in dealing with children that goes far beyond sentimental love. Nearly all leisure activities include some educational aspects. For Europeans and North Americans this is not unusual – you'll feel at home.

There's only one thing here where Cuba is very different: the lack of toys has to be compensated by imagination. But that isn't such a bad thing surely – maybe it's even a good remedy for the consumer pressures ruling children's lives at home.

HAVANA

ISLA DEL COCO ● (130 A2) (*⊞ D2*)
Aparatos imported from China such as the *Montaña Rusa* (roller coaster), swings and slides and lots more to guarantee hours of fun and multicultural encounters without any language barriers at this theme and fun park in the capital. *5a Av./C/ 112 | Miramar | Wed–Sun 10am–6pm | admission 1 Peso*

Photo: Family scene in Parque Cespedes, Santiago de Cuba

Lions, Indians, dinos and crocs, cave adventures, beaches – and again and again, playgrounds with funny carousels

JARDÍN ZOO DE LA HABANA

(130 A2) (*W D2*)

Although the zoo's animal welfare standards are not the highest (tigers are kept in a concrete floor cage), the children love watching the chimpanzees and the playground. *Av. 26/Av. Zoológico | Tue–Sun 9am–5.30pm | admission 2, children up to 12 years of age 1 CUC*

PARQUE LENÍN (130 A2) (*W D2*)

There are lots of things for children to explore in this 7.5 km²/2.9 sq miles large, slightly overgrown park in the south of Havana: the *Parque Zoológico Nacional (Wed–Sun 10am–3pm | admission 3, children 2 CUC)* INSIDER TIP with pony rides and petting zoo, the *Jardín Botánico Nacional (Wed–Sun 10am–4pm | admission 4, children 3 CUC)* with many exotic plants and the Japanese garden as well as the fun park *Parque Mariposa (Thu–Sun 10am–5pm)*. Access via Av. de Independencia and Av. de San Francisco *(signposted)*

Cuban children know what to look for: the cocoa fruits

departs for a 45-min trip on the Río Canimar to the shore ranch of *La Arboleda*. After having lunch there, you're free to go on a horseback hack or trip in a rowing boat, until it's time to head back, at 4.30pm. *Ctra. Varadero–Matanzas | tel. 45 26 15 16 | adults 45, children 22.50 CUC*

CUEVA DEL INDIO (128 C3) (*ℳ C2*)
A true cave adventure: first 250 m/275 yd into the mountain on foot, then on by boat, and out again the other side. *Valle de Viñales | daily 9am–5.30pm | 5 CUC, children up to the age of 10 go free*

CUEVAS DE BELLAMAR ●
(130 B2) (*ℳ E2*)
Cuba's largest cave can be visited here underground. Although its exact measurement is unknown, the cave is reportedly over 11 km/6.8 miles long; it also boasts stalagmites up to 12 m/39 ft in height which can be seen in the visitors' section. *Ctra. a la Cuevas | Matanzas | daily 9am–5pm | admission 5 CUC, Tour de las Esponias (im unbeleuchteten Teil) 8 CUC, children up to 12 years of age 6 CUC*

MUSEO PROVINCIAL
(130 B2) (*ℳ E2*)
One attraction has to be observed under the magnifying glass: INSIDER TIP two preserved fleas that have been dressed in clothes. There's a 130-year old mummy and other bizarre things too. *C/ Magdalena/Milanés | Matanzas | Tue–Sat 9.30am–noon and 1–5pm, Sun 9am–noon | admission 2 CUC*

THE WEST

LA BOCA/GUAMÁ (130 B–C3) (*ℳ E–F3*)
On the *crocodile farm (daily 9.30am–5pm | admission 5 CUC)* in La Boca, daring crocodile tamers show off their talents and gigantic native Cuban crocodiles can be seen – behind bars of course.. And children will love the 32 life-like sculptures of Indians by Rita Longa in *Guamá. Departures in La Boca | 12 CUC, children 5 CUC | Peninsula de Zapata*

BOAT TRIP ON THE RÍO CANIMAR
(130 C2) (*ℳ F2*)
Every day at noon, at the *Parque Turístico Canimar* below the bridge, a boat

THE CENTRE

JUNGLE TOUR (132 C1) (*ℳ J2–3*)
An exploration of the mangrove maze of Cayo Guillermo with its many wild animals by motorboat is not only exciting for children, the parents too will enjoy

this a lot! *Marina Cayo Guillermo | adults 39, children 19.50 CUC*

MORÓN (132 C2) *(ᗢ J3)*

Enjoy a day away from the beach and book a boat trip to the *Laguna de Redonda (14 km/8.6 miles north of Morón)*. 5 km/2.6 miles south east is the *Museo de Azúcar (admission for adults 10 CUC, children 6 CUC)* with old steam engines on display. In the town itself, children are allowed to climb up the town's landmark, its large cockerel!

SITIO LA GÜIRA (132 C1) *(ᗢ K3)*

A great day out, especially for city kids, is the farm at Cayo Coco with free-running hens, turkeys, ducks and horses and a beautiful garden. You can also spend the night in one of the no-frills huts for a real adventure *(Budget)*; remember to pack mosquito nets and cream! *Ctra. a Cayo Guillermo, km 10 | Tel. 33 30 12 08*

THE EAST

ACUARIO CAYO NARANJO
(134 C3) *(ᗢ N4–5)*

The fun starts with the crossing, as the basins for the dolphins and other sea creatures lie on an island in Naranjo Bay which you can only reach by boat. The biggest attraction is the possibility to swim with dolphins. *Ctra. Guardalavaca, km 48 | daily 9am–4.30pm | admission incl. boat transfer 89, children 49 CUC, 75/37 CUC incl. swimming with dolphins*

ALDEA TAÍNA (134 C3) *(ᗢ N5)*

With war paint, loincloths and headbands around their long black hair, these "Indians" look pretty authentic; they perform their dances for groups (of at least 10). Ask at the hotel whether enough people are interested. *Ctra. a Banes | daily 9am–4pm | admission to village 5 CUC*

PLAZA DE MARTE (134 C5) *(ᗢ N6)*

Santiago's pretty square transforms into an enormous playground and meeting point for families on Sundays. Your children will quickly find someone to play with. The enormous fun park *Parque de los Sueños* on the Carretera Siboney *(Wed–Sun 10am–6pm, have pesos at the ready)* also offers fun for all the family.

VALLE DE LA PREHISTORIA
(135 D5) *(ᗢ O5)*

Mammoths, sabre-tooth tigers, tyrannosaurus rex – in this pre-historic valley, dino fans won't know where to look first. All 227 figures are life-size. *Ctra. a Baconao, km 6.5 | daily 8am–5pm | admission 1, children 0.50 CUC*

Enchanted: entrance of the Cueva del Indio

FESTIVALS & EVENTS

Cuba likes to party with a high artistic standard. Various festivals have an excellent international reputation, most of all the International Festival of New Latin American film in Havana, which takes place in December. Party in true Caribbean style at the various carnivals organized in cities throughout the year, the craziest being held on July 26 in Santiago de Cuba. Since the latest popes visited the island, Good Friday and Christmas have returned as holidays on Cuba. More cultural information (in Spanish): *www. ministeriodecultura.gob.cu*, *cubaescena. cult.cu* (theatre, dance), events calendar in English at *www.lahabana.com*.

NATIONAL HOLIDAYS

1 January	Liberation Day
28 January	José Martí's birthday
24 February	Commemoration of the war of independence
8 March	International Women's Day
March/April	Good Friday
19 April	Victory in the Bay of Pigs
1 May	Labour Day
26 July	Day of the storming of the Moncada barracks
30 July	Day of the martyrs of the revolution
8 October	Capturing of Che Guevara
10 October	Start of the first war of independence
28 October	Disappearance of Camilo Cienfuego
25 December	Christmas
31 December	New Year's Eve

EVENTS

JANUARY
LIV Premio Literario Casa de las Américas: The renowned literary prize is awarded to American writers in Havana; *www.casadelasamericas.org*

FEBRUARY
Feria internacional del libro: International book exhibition held in Havana and many other locations around Cuba; *www.cubarte.cult.cu* (in Spanish)

MARCH
Concurso internacional para estudiantes de ballet: International competition for ballet students held in Havana

Not just any old fiestas – carnival and famous festivals add colour to the revolutionary calendar of events

APRIL

Festival Internacional de Cine Pobre de Humberto Solás: Festival for films which cost less than 300,000 US$, shown in Gibara; *ficgibara.cult.cu*

MAY

Torneo Internacional de la Pesca de la Aguja "Ernest Hemingway": fishing competition, initiated in 1950 by Ernest Hemingway; *www.nauticamarlin.com*

JUNE

Carnival in Camagüey, Trinidad and Varadero – usually held on the last weekend of the month

JULY

Festival del Caribe: music and dance in Santiago de Cuba; culminating at the end of the month in the ★ *Carnival*

JULY/AUGUST

Carnival in Havana: masks, floats, music, grandstands on the Malecón

SEPTEMBER

Nuestra Señora de la Caridad del Cobre: On the name day of their patron saint, September 8, many Cubans visit her pilgrimage site at the Iglesia of El Cobre

OCTOBER

Festival de Teatro de la Habana: Theatre festival in Havana (every 2 years, next one in 2019); *www.cubaescena.cult.cu*

NOVEMBER

Musikfestival Beny Moré: The singer (1919–63) is celebrated in his home town of Santa Isabel (near Cienfuegos).

DECEMBER

★ *Festival Internacional del Nuevo Cine Latinoamericano:* International Festival of Latin American film in Havana; *habanafilmfestival.com*

INSIDER TIP *Parrandas:* carnivalesque processions in Remedios (16 and 24)

Regatta Felíz Navidad: Christmas regatta in Havana to end the year

LINKS, BLOGS, APPS & MORE

LINKS & BLOGS

www.travel2cuba.co.uk Metasite giving a good overview of Cuba's most important destinations, marinas, diving sites and golf courses. There are photo galleries that show the island's architecture, nature and cultural sights as well as beaches. A handy list of tour operators will make travel planning even easier.

www.cuba.cu The state-official Cuba website (in Spanish): provides information (weather, events etc.) as well as an advertising platform for products and politi-

cal parties. The *Reflexiones del Comandante en Jefe Fidel Castro Ruz* are also published on this site. Links available on science, culture, sport, education, health, tourism, politics and economy

www.biography.com/people/fidel-castro-9241487 Get past the ad, and find an in-depth exploration of Fidel Castro's biography

www.cubarte.cult.cu Interested in the arts? If you have a smattering of Spanish, will find up-to-date information on current events. Also eminently helpful: the collection of links under *Portales*

www.lahabana.com Nicely presented online magazine that goes beyond basic information for travellers by posting some in-depth features on Cuban society and history, on music and the arts scene

www.14ymedio.com Cuban online daily newspaper (English language version also available) posting blogs from the well-known Cuban journalists Yoani Sánchez and Reinaldo Escobar

www.gettingstamped.com/guide-for-americans-traveling-to-cuba-2016 Travelling to Cuba is just a tiny bit more complicated for US citizens – this guide is a great starting point!

www.goatsontheroad.com/category/blogs/cuba This travel blog by Canadian couple Nick and Dariece has a whole collection of posts about travelling Cuba. Anyone wanting to make the

most of their holiday budget will find the posts about backpacking Cuba, the couple's travel cost breakdown and *casas particulares* most interesting.

generacionyen.wordpress.com English translation of the fascinating and comprehensive blog by a young female intellectual dissident on the very real limitations on women's lives on Cuba

www.cubaforums.com Tourist reviews, recommendations & discussions of Cuba's hotels, resorts, transport, culture and general travel advice

VIDEOS & MUSIC

vimeo.com/9896852, 58011206 and 32374965 Three very atmospheric videos, placing the focus on the inhabitants of Havana's Old Town and giving them a beautiful, poetically inspired stage. In only three to four minutes, those clips manage to provide a deep insight into Cuban life; in HD quality

www.youtube.com/watch?v=GbXaVIdb2rI Short documentary about Cuba's food revolution. As the country is changing, Cuba's culinary scene is catching up. The interviews tell of challenges, like unsteady ingredient supply and shaky internet connections, but also show how Cuban traditions and ingenuity create deliciousness

www.youtube.com/channel/UCulIPhX8Jyz2FnT8AeMRO8g The YouTube channel of Addicted2Salsa has various great instruction videos for salsa beginners. www.youtube.com/watch?v=YwxB1MSytYA by Dance Papi shows how to dance the basic step, called Guapea, of Cuban salsa

www.youtube.com/watch?v=dHBkLj5Bbq4 A day in the life of Havana: a good 10-minute introduction to Cuba's capital

APPS

www.havescotchwilltravel.com/best-cuba-aps With the internet not always being easily accessible in Cuba, having a few helpful apps for offline use will make travelling the island a breeze. We definitely recommend getting at least an offline map like the one by Applantation

Congas & Bongos A rhythm once started you can never stop: bongo percussions on the (Android) mobile create Cuba feeling everywhere

TRAVEL TIPS

ARRIVAL

International airlines such as Air France or Iberia usually only land in Havana and Varadero, while charter companies servicing the major package operators also fly to Cayo Coco, Santa Clara, Camagüey and Holguín. Flights can be had from 630 £ (last-minute remaining seats for short stays) from London. At immigration, holidaymakers need to show a passport that is at least 6 months valid still and a tourist card (currently £20/US$30). This also applies to children who require a children's ID card with photo. Individual travellers receive the card from specialised operators (e. g. together with their flight booking) or by post from the Cuban embassy (cheque plus stamped return envelope). For package tourists this is usually included in the holiday price. At immigration, you also have to show health insurance protection that is valid on Cuba. When leaving the country, the copy of the tourist card has to be handed back. The former „departure tax" of 25 CUC in cash doesn't exist as such anymore, it is now included in the ticket price. Unless entering Cuba from a third country such as Canada, Mexico or the Bahamas, US citizens can only travel to Cuba with a licence issued by the Department of Treasury.

BUSES

The modern and air-conditioned buses of *Viazul* run between all cities on Cuba and are usually even on time. The journey from Havana to Varadero, for instance, costs 10 CUC. Prices and routes are listed under *www.viazul.com* which also offers online bookings. Address and bus station in Havana: *Av. 26/Zoológico | tel. 78 81 14 13.* With the slogan *Conectando Cuba* (connecting Cuba), modern buses also shuttle guests between the various hotels in Cuba for the same price as the *Viazul* buses. Ask at your reception for more information. The hop-on hop-off sightseeing buses can also be found in the tourist resorts of Viñales, Havana, Varadero or Trinidad. Tickets cost 5–10 CUC.

CAR HIRE

No international car rental firms are active on Cuba. If you want to book at good rates, talk to a specialised operator or book directly via *www.cubatravel network.com*. For 5 days expect to pay 60 CUC. On the island insurance of 15 CUC/day is added. Drivers (at least 21 years of age) have to show a national licence, their credit card will be swiped as security, and they often have to pay

RESPONSIBLE TRAVEL

It doesn't take a lot to be environmentally friendly whilst travelling. Don't just think about your carbon footprint whilst flying to and from your holiday destination but also about how you can protect nature and culture abroad. As a tourist it is especially important to respect nature, look out for local products, cycle instead of driving, save water and much more. If you would like to find out more about eco-tourism please visit: *www.ecotourism.org*

for the first tankful (keep the receipt!). Additional drivers cost 3 CUC/day and are registered. Check whether the spare wheel fits (if not, you might be asked to cough up at a later date for one that fits). If an inspection is due on the vehicle and you don't take it to a branch of the car hire company, you will be forced to pay a fine *(multa)*. If your car has a puncture, drive with your spare tyre to a *gomero*. The mechanic will repair the tyre for circa 20 CUC. Change a flat tyre immediately to protect the wheel rims. To curb drinking while driving, it is forbidden to transport alcohol in cars. In the holiday centres you can hire scooters; in Varadero for instance for 25 CUC/day (plus 25 CUC security).

CLIMATE, WHEN TO GO

On Cuba the sun shines all year round. In the winter months (the dry season) the nights are colder than in summer, and a few days might be cold too. If you don't like high levels of humidity, visit in the dry season (mid-November to April). The other months are the rainy season. During that time hurricanes may sweep Cuba, in particular between late August and late October. In the acute threat of a hurricane, follow the instructions of your travel rep or host.

CONSULATES & EMBASSIES

EMBASSIES OF THE REPUBLIC OF CUBA (INTEREST SECTION IN THE US)
– *167 High Holborn | London WC1V 6PA | UK | tel. 020 72 40 24 88 | consulcuba@ uk.embacuba.cu | misiones.minrex.gob. cu/en/united-kingdom*

– *2630 16th Street NW| Washington DC | 20009 | tel. (+1)202 797 85 18 20 | recep cion@usadc.embacuba.cu | misiones. minrex.gob.cu/en/usa*

UK EMBASSY
C/ 34 No. 702e/7ma | Miramar, Playa | Habana | tel. 07 21 42 22 00 | UkinCuba@ fco.gov.uk | www.gov.uk/world/cuba

US INTEREST SECTION
Calzada between L&M Streets | Vedado |

BUDGETING

Dance show from	£65/US$ 93
	e.g. at the Tropicana
Coffee	£0.65–1.30/US$ 0.90–1.90
	for a cup
Cigar	£6.15/US$ 8.70
	for a Cohiba by Robaina
Chocolate	£0.75/US$ 1.05
	250 g from Baracoa
Petrol	£1.05/US$ 1.50
	for a litre of super unleaded
Cocktail	from £2.60/US$ 3.70
	for a Cuba libre or mojíto in a bar

Habana | tel. 7839-4100 | havanaconsu larinfo@state.gov | cu.usembassy.gov

CUSTOMS

You are permitted to bring items for personal use into Cuba, but no pornographic magazines, animal and plant products or electrical appliances. You may not export books that were published over 50 years ago in Cuba, crayfish or art – unless you have the requisite export permits with stamp; for more than 50 cigars you need the receipt and a certificate of authenticity. Information: *www.aduana.co.cu*. Entering a EU country from Cuba, you may bring 200 cigarettes or 100 cigarillos or 50 cigars or 250 g of tobacco; 1 l of spirits; or 2 l of alcoholic drinks no more than 22 % vol.; also goods with a value of up to £390. With the US, the situation is more complex, see www.aduana.co.cu.

DOMESTIC FLIGHTS

To get a seat on a domestic flight, you have to book at least four weeks ahead. The Havana–Santiago de Cuba connection (800 km/500 miles as the crow flies) is particularly in demand; return tickets with Cubana from £240/US$340. *Cubana de Aviación office: C/ 23 no. 64/ corner C/ Infanta | Vedado | Havana | tel. 78 34 44 46 | www.cubana.cu | Aerocaribbean: www.cubajet.com*

ELECTRICITY

More recent hotels have European 220-volt power points, all others American 110-volt electric sockets. Bring an adapter!

EMERGENCY

The police emergency number in all of Cuba is 106; the central number if you've lost your credit card is *119 49 11 61 16*.

HEALTH

No vaccinations are required, unless you enter Cuba from a country where cholera or yellow fever is prevalent. For Ebola prevention, arriving passengers must fill in a health questionnaire. Be careful with water, to avoid stomach or gastric disturbances. Recommended vaccinations include diphtheria, hepatitis A and tetanus. You should have all the medication you need with you in sufficient quantity. The major tourist hotels have first-aid stations, usually staffed by a doctor, in the tourist areas also international clinics (*www.servimed cuba.com* or contact your embassy). If you need medical attention, pay in cash in CUC. Proof of an existing travel health insurance (in Spanish!) is obligatory to enter Cuba!

INFORMATION

CUBAN TOURISM AUTHORITY
Cuba Tourist Office (Embassy of Cuba), 167 High Holborn | London WC1V 6PA | United Kingdom | tel. 020 72 40 66 55 | tourism@travel2cuba.co.uk | www.cuba. travel.com/en

1200 Bay St., Suite 305 | Toronto Ontario M5R 2A5 | Canada | tel. 1-416-362-0700 | www.cuba.travel.com/en and www.go cuba.ca

INTERNET

Virtually every town and city now has a WiFi hotspot, mainly located in a public park. The state-owned telephone company *Etecsa* sells internet access cards for 2–7 CUC (1–5 hrs). Those who prefer to go online from a PC rather than from their smartphone should use the *Etecsa* office terminals. Be warned though: the connection is slow.

MONEY & CURRENCY

So far, Cuba's economy works with two currencies (this is due to end soon): the

Cuban peso (CUP or MN) and the peso convertible (CUC), the Cuban exchange currency, which is worthless abroad. Now you may exchange US dollars in bureaux de change or banks into CUC, though you'll pay a ten per cent fee! Euro is accepted as a payment currency in most tourist centres. The best option is to travel with euros in cash as well as with a European VISA or MasterCard credit card (credit cards issued by US banks and the Maestro debit card are not accepted anywhere on Cuba!). The CUC dual currency is available from banks with a credit card and passport provided as a proof of identity. A 3% commission fee will be charged for this transaction. All you need is a (European) VISA credit card with pin number to draw CUC out of many of the ATM machines – provided they are not out of order. Careful though: if you lose your Eurocard/MasterCard, no replacement can be sent to Cuba. In February 2018, 1 peso convertible (CUC) was worth 25 Cuban pesos (CUP). The national currency can be used by tourists to shop on the farmers markets or at snack stalls.

PERSONAL SAFETY

Cuba always had the reputation of being the safest place to travel in South America. However since the country's divide between its poor and rich (successful self-employed Cubans) has widened, theft on the island is more common and there are also reports about attacks on tourists. Be careful in lonely areas and with touts who might recommend private accommodation.

PHONE & MOBILE PHONE

International calls to landlines from a state-owned *Etecsa* office cost 1.50 CUC a minute (0.45 CUC a minute for national calls and 0.35 CUC for mobiles). Etecsa also sells national and international phone cards which you can only use in certain public telephones. It makes more sense to buy a cheap Cuban pre-paid mobile (from 25 CUC, you need your passport for the contract) which you can then recharge in any *Etecsa* office. For calls abroad, the dialling code is 119, then the country code (UK 44, Ireland 353, USA 01), then the local dialling call without the zero. Dialling code for Cuba: 0053. For domestic calls, enter the local dialling code directly followed by the number of the person you are calling (removing the zero) and the numbers in

CURRENCY CONVERTER

£	CUC	CUC	£
1	1.41	1	0.71
2	2.83	2	1.42
3	4.24	3	2.12
4	5.65	4	2.83
5	7.06	5	3.54
7	9.88	6	4.25
8	11.31	7	4.95
9	12.72	8	5.66
10	14.13	9	6.37

$	CUC	CUC	$
1	1	1	1
2	2	2	2
3	3	3	3
4	4	4	4
5	5	5	5
7	7	6	6
8	8	7	7
9	9	8	8
10	10	9	9

For current exchange rates see www.xe.com

this guide. When making calls between mobile phones, simply enter the mobile phone number (all numbers start with 05).

European mobile/cell phones with a contract will automatically switch to the roaming partner Cubacel. Cubacel also offers pre-paid chips; cost: installation fee of 8 CUC plus minimum credits of 5 CUC plus 3 CUC for each day connected.

POST

Stamps can usually be bought together with postcards in the shops, at post offices and in some Etecsa (telephone) offices. An airmail postcard to international destinations costs 0.75 CUC. Mail to the US still travels via Canada or Mexico.

PRIVATE ACCOMMODATION

Casas particulares (private houses) are a good-value alternative to the state-run hotels and allow contact with the locals. Addresses and information: *www.cubacasas.net, www.casaparticularcuba.org.* Private accommodation and apartments in Cuba can now be booked via *www.airbnb.com.* You can read the feedback and ratings on the B&Bs at *www.tripadvisor.com.* You'll recognise *casas particulares* by a white sign with a dark-blue icon in the shape of a vertical anchor, usually stuck to the door entrance.

TAXI

The trip from Havana airport into the city costs approx. 25 CUC. The vintage taxis

WEATHER IN HAVANA

	Jan	Feb	March	April	May	June	July	Aug	Sept	Oct	Nov	Dec
Daytime temperatures in °C/°F	26/79	27/81	28/82	29/84	30/86	31/88	31/88	32/90	31/88	29/84	27/81	26/79
Nighttime temperatures in °C/°F	18/64	18/64	19/66	21/70	22/72	23/73	24/75	24/75	24/75	23/73	21/70	19/66
☀ Sunshine hours/day	6	6	7	7	8	6	6	6	5	5	5	5
☂ Precipitation days/month	6	4	4	4	7	10	9	10	11	11	7	6
≈ Water temperature in °C/°F	25/77	24/75	24/75	26/79	27/81	27/81	28/82	28/82	28/82	28/82	27/81	27/81

☀ Sunshine hours/day ☂ Precipitation days/month ≈ Water temperature in °C/°F

have no taximeter and the fare has to be negotiated. While all other taxis are legally obliged to use the taximeter, many drivers like to switch it off. *Taxis particulares* are private taxis (negotiate the price before you set off); *taxis colectivos* are mainly reserved for Cubans and travel fixed routes for prices in peso; you should also agree on the price with the driver beforehand.

TIME

To align with Cuban time, turn the clock back 5 hours compared to Britain.

TIPPING

Instead of making the meagre Cuban salaries the yardstick for your tipping policy, it's better to use international standards: 2 CUC for carrying luggage, for example.

TOUR OPERATORS

A list of British tour operators that go to Cuba can be found here: *www.travel2cuba.co.uk/cuba-tour-operators.* Swiss Cuba specialist *Caribbean Tours* (see p. 47) runs an office on Cuba *(Av. Paseo 606 | betw. C/ 25 and 27 | Vedado | tel. 7 8 34 42 51)*. Eagle Activities, among other operators, offer salsa holidays on Cuba: *www.eagleactivities.co.uk/holidays/type/cuba*

TRAFFIC

Cuba drives on the right. Drivers frequently hog the overtaking lane to avoid the many horse-drawn carriages, bikes and pedestrians on the right-hand side of the roads. On country roads maximum 80 km/h is allowed, on the motorway (if not otherwise signalled) 100

km/h, in built-up areas 50 km/h. *Punto de Control* means checkpoint; make sure you go down to the prescribed 40 km/h! When parking always look for secured spaces *(parqueos)* or look for somebody to guard the car (and pay him). With accidents (or theft), everything has to be noted and logged by the police for the insurance to pay out. Ask for a copy of the log and make a note of the name of the police officer. Night drives carry a major risk of accidents, as people, animals and cars with no lights may be travelling on the roads. Speeding may entail a penalty *(multa)*. However, the police may not take money off drivers; they have to log the fine in the rental car agreement. If involved in an accident where a person is harmed, a tourist has to stay in the country until the recuperation of the injured party is foreseeable or their medical or hospital bills have been paid. The modern "Servi" stations are open day and night. A litre of *especial* (super unleaded) costs 1.20 CUC. You practically always have to pay in cash, even if the petrol station is covered in credit card stickers claiming they are accepted there.

TRAINS

The railway network is approx. 9,300 km/5779 miles long and operates all the major cities. The best train in terms of comfort is the *tren especial.* It often takes a long time to get from A to B and departing times are irregular (see *www.hicuba.com/ferrocarril.htm*). In Havana, trains are currently arriving and departing from the small terminal *La Coubre (between main station and port)* due to renovations on the large station.

USEFUL PHRASES SPANISH

PRONUNCIATION

c	before "e" and "i" like "th" in "thin"
ch	as in English
g	before "e" and "i" like the "ch" in Scottish "loch"
gue, gui	like "get", "give"
que, qui	the "u" is not spoken, i.e. "ke", "ki"
j	always like the "ch" in Scottish "loch"
ll	like "lli" in "million"; some speak it like "y" in "yet"
ñ	"nj"
z	like "th" in "thin"

IN BRIEF

Yes/No/Maybe	sí/no/quizás
Please/Thank you	por favor/gracias
Hello!/Goodbye!/See you	¡Hola!/¡Adiós!/¡Hasta luego!
Good morning!/afternoon!/evening!/night!	¡Buenos días!/¡Buenos días!/¡Buenas tardes!/¡Buenas noches!
Excuse me, please!	¡Perdona!/¡Perdone!
May I...?/Pardon?	¿Puedo...?/¿Cómo dice?
My name is...	Me llamo...
What's your name?	¿Cómo se llama usted?/¿Cómo te llamas?
I'm from...	Soy de...
I would like to .../Have you got ...?	Querría .../¿Tiene usted ...?
How much is...?	¿Cuánto cuesta...?
I (don't) like that	Esto (no) me gusta.
good/bad/broken/doesn't work	bien/mal/roto/no funciona
too much/much/little/all/nothing	demasiado/mucho/poco/todo/nada
Help!/Attention!/Caution!	¡Socorro!/¡Atención!/¡Cuidado!
ambulance/police/fire brigade	ambulancia/policía/bomberos
May I take a photo here	¿Podría fotografiar aquí?

DATE & TIME

Monday/Tuesday/Wednesday	lunes/martes/miércoles
Thursday/Friday/Saturday	jueves/viernes/sábado
Sunday/working day/holiday	domingo/laborable/festivo
today/tomorrow/yesterday	hoy/mañana/ayer

¿Hablas español?

"Do you speak Spanish?" This guide will help you to say the basic words and phrases in Spanish

hour/minute/second/moment	hora/minuto/segundo/momento
day/night/week/month/year	día/noche/semana/mes/año
now/immediately/before/after	ahora/enseguida/antes/después
What time is it?	¿Qué hora es?
It's three o'clock/It's half past three	Son las tres/Son las tres y media
a quarter to four/a quarter past four	cuatro menos cuarto/ cuatro y cuarto

TRAVEL

open/closed/opening times	abierto/cerrado/horario
entrance / exit	entrada/acceso salida
departure/arrival	salida/llegada
toilets/ladies/gentlemen	aseos/señoras/caballeros
free/occupied	libre/ocupado
(not) drinking water	agua (no) potable
Where is...?/Where are...?	¿Dónde está...? /¿Dónde están...?
left/right	izquierda/derecha
straight ahead/back	recto/atrás
close/far	cerca/lejos
traffic lights/corner/crossing	semáforo/esquina/cruce
bus/tram/U-underground/	autobús/tranvía/metro/
taxi/cab	taxi
bus stop/cab stand	parada/parada de taxis
parking lot/parking garage	parking/garaje
street map/map	plano de la ciudad/mapa
train station/harbour/airport	estación/puerto/aeropuerto
ferry/quay	transbordador/muelle
schedule/ticket/supplement	horario/billete/suplemento
single/return	sencillo/ida y vuelta
train/track/platform	tren/vía/andén
delay/strike	retraso/huelga
I would like to rent...	Querría... alquilar
a car/a bicycle/a boat	un coche/una bicicleta/un barco
petrol/gas station	gasolinera
petrol/gas / diesel	gasolina/diesel
breakdown/repair shop	avería/taller

FOOD & DRINK

Could you please book a table for tonight for four?	Resérvenos, por favor, una mesa para cuatro personas para hoy por la noche.
on the terrace/by the window	en la terraza/junto a la ventana

The menu, please/	¡El menú, por favor!
Could I please have...?	¿Podría traerme... por favor?
bottle/carafe/glass	botella/jarra/vaso
knife/fork/spoon	cuchillo/tenedor/cuchara
salt/pepper/sugar	sal/pimienta/azúcar
vinegar/oil/milk/cream/lemon	vinagre/aceite/leche/limón
cold/too salty/not cooked	frío/demasiado salado/sin hacer
with/without ice/sparkling	con/sin hielo/gas
vegetarian/allergy	vegetariano/vegetariana/alergía
May I have the bill, please?	Querría pagar, por favor.
bill/receipt/tip	cuenta/recibo/propina

SHOPPING

pharmacy/chemist	farmacia/droguería
baker/market	panadería/mercado
butcher/fishmonger	carnicería/pescadería
shopping centre/department store	centro comercial/grandes almacenes
shop/supermarket/kiosk	tienda/supermercado/quiosco
100 grammes/1 kilo	cien gramos/un kilo
expensive/cheap/price/more/less	caro/barato/precio/más/menos
organically grown	de cultivo ecológico

ACCOMMODATION

I have booked a room	He reservado una habitación.
Do you have any ... left?	¿Tiene todavía ...?
single room/double room	habitación individual/habitación doble
breakfast/half board/	desayuno/media pensión/
full board (American plan)	pensión completa
at the front/seafront/garden view	hacia delante/hacia el mar/hacia el jardín
shower/sit-down bath	ducha/baño
balcony/terrace	balcón/terraza
key/room card	llave/tarjeta
luggage/suitcase/bag	equipaje/maleta/bolso
swimming pool/spa/sauna	piscina/spa/sauna
soap/toilet paper/nappy (diaper)	jabón/papel higiénico/pañal
cot/high chair/nappy changing	cuna/trona/cambiar los pañales
deposit	anticipo/caución

BANKS, MONEY & CREDIT CARDS

bank/ATM/	banco/cajero automático/
pin code	número secreto
cash/credit card	en efectivo/tarjeta de crédito
bill/coin/change	billete/moneda/cambio

HEALTH

doctor/dentist/paediatrician	médico/dentista/pediatra
hospital/emergency clinic	hospital/urgencias
fever/pain/inflamed/injured	fiebre/dolor/inflamado/herido
diarrhoea/nausea/sunburn	diarrea/náusea/quemadura de sol
plaster/bandage/ointment/cream	tirita/vendaje/pomada/crema
painkiller/tablet/suppository	calmante/comprimido/supositorio

POST, TELECOMMUNICATIONS & MEDIA

stamp/letter/postcard	sello/carta/postal
I need a landline phone card/	Necesito una tarjeta telefónica/
I'm looking for a prepaid card for my mobile	Busco una tarjeta prepago para mi móvil
Where can I find internet access?	¿Dónde encuentro un acceso a internet?
dial/connection/engaged	marcar/conexión/ocupado
socket/adapter/charger	enchufe/adaptador/cargador
computer/battery/ rechargeable battery	ordenador/batería/ batería recargable
e-mail address/at sign (@)	(dirección de) correo electrónico/arroba
internet address (URL)	dirección de internet
internet connection/wifi	conexión a internet/wifi
e-mail/file/print	archivo/imprimir

LEISURE, SPORTS & BEACH

beach/sunshade/lounger	playa/sombrilla/tumbona
low tide/high tide/current	marea baja/marea alta/corriente

NUMBERS

0	cero	14	catorce
1	un, uno, una	15	quince
2	dos	16	dieciséis
3	tres	17	diecisiete
4	cuatro	18	dieciocho
5	cinco	19	diecinueve
6	seis	20	veinte
7	siete	100	cien, ciento
8	ocho	200	doscientos, doscientas
9	nueve	1000	mil
10	diez	2000	dos mil
11	once	10000	diez mil
12	doce	1/2	medio
13	trece	1/4	un cuarto

ROAD ATLAS

The green line indicates the Discovery Tour "Cuba at a glance"
The blue line indicates the other Discovery Tours

All tours are also marked on the pull-out map

Photo: Cayo Santa María

Exploring Cuba

The map on the back cover shows how the area has been sub-divided

A **B** **C**

1

Gulf *of* *Mex*

Tropic of Cancer

Golfo *de* *Mé*

2

2000

1166

A r c h i p i é l a g o d e l o s C o l o r a d o s

Cayo Inés
de Soto

Man
Sangu

3 **Pinar del Río**

La
Esperanza

San Cayetano

Sta. Lucia

*Cuevas
del Indio*

*Cuevas
Josef*

Pta. Tabaco

Minas
de Matahambre

14

Viñales

*Sa. de
Sa-nlos*

Valle de
Viñales

San Ramon

Dimas

110

591

Cabeza

Cayos de
Buenavista

*P.N. los
Organos*

**PINAR
DEL RÍO**

S. Carlos

*Emb.
el Punto*

21

4

Arroyos
de Mantua

Sa. de los Organos

Mantua

Pta. de
la Sierra

San Luis

Las Clavellinas

*Golfo de
Guanahacabibes*

Guane

363

CC

S. Juan
y Martínez

34

Cd. Bolivar

Isabel
Rubio

Ensenada de Cortés

B. de Guadiana

La Fé

25

Sandino

Cortés

Carabelita

*Pen. de
Guanahacabibes*

Manuel Lazo

Las Martinas

P.N. Cayos

Bolondron

El Beral

La
Bajada

*Bahía
de
Corrientes*

Maria la
Gorda

*P.N. Península
de Guanahacabibes*

C. de S. Antonio

C. Corrientes

5

Y u c a t a n

2000

2451

C h a n n e l

6

30 km
18.64 mi

4000

4820

128

5055

D **E** **F**

1

c o
1648
714

i c o
2343

LA HABANA
(HAVANA)
La Habana

Tarara Sta. Ma. del Mar
Guanabo
35 104
C. Florido C. Cienfu
Guanabacoa C. Cienfu Sta. Cr
S. José
d.l.Lajas Caraballo
Cotorro 58
Playa Baracoa Santa Fé Caimito Catalina Ag
HAV d.G Mad
San Bejucal 67
Alturas de Bejucal-Madruga-Coliseo 278
Antonio d.l.B Güines Cal
Guira S.Felipe 56 Vegas
de Melena Melena S.
d.Sur Nicolas 45
Batabanó Playa
Surgidero Rosario Playa del
de Batabanó Caimito

Bahía de Cabañas
Quiebra Hacha
Cabañas Mariel Bahía
Bahía
Honda CN
Guanajay 32 23
Cayajabos 13
Soroa **90**
P.N. La Güira 35 Artemisa Alquizar El
San Diego **A4** Candelaria Majana Junco
d.l.B Candelaria S.Cristobal 44 Guanimar Playa **Mayabeque**
Taco Taco S.Juan El Cajío
Los El **Artemisa** Cayeria
Paso Real Palacios Francés las Cayamas Ensenada
70 de S.Diego El de-la-Broa
ión Cubanacán Pinar *Golfo de*
Sur S. Diego Playa *Batabanó* Crocodile
Tablazo Dayaniguas 6 Farm
Alonso de Rojas *Cayos del* **4**
Honda *Hambre* *Cayería de*
Aguas Claras *Diego Pérez*

ayos
n Felipe
elipe Nueva *Cayo*
Cayos La Gerona *San Juan*
los Indios Demajagua El Abra 295 **Isla de la Juventud**
La Melvis Júcaro *Cayo*
Ensenada 310 J9 La Fé *Cantiles* **5**
de la La Reforma
Singuanea Argelia Julia A. Mella
C. Francés Libre Cayo Piedra
rino Punta Francés Siguanea P. N. Pta.
Jacksonville *Ciénaga* del-Este *Cayo Palma* Cayo Largo
de Lanier Rincón
del Guanal
Isla de la Juventud
(Isla de Pinos)
Archipiélago d e   l o s   C a n a r r e o s **6**

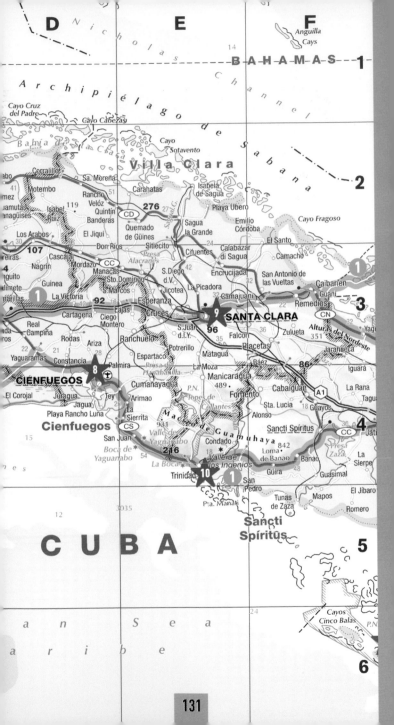

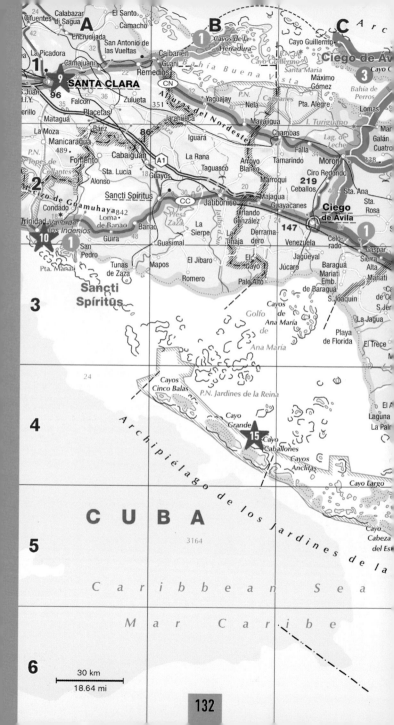

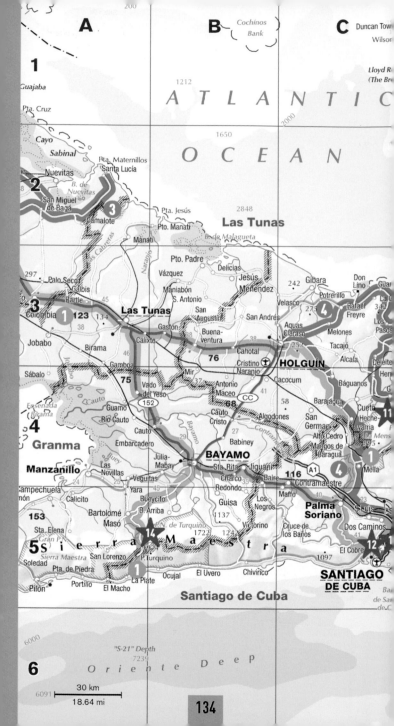

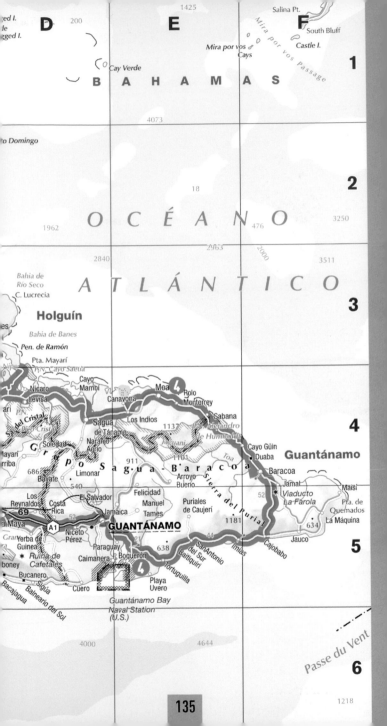

KEY TO ROAD ATLAS

German	Symbol	French / Spanish
Autobahn, mehrspurige Straße - in Bau Highway, multilane divided road - under construction		Autoroute, route à plusieurs voies - en construction Autopista, carretera de más carriles - en construcción
Fernverkehrsstraße - in Bau Trunk road - under construction		Route à grande circulation - en construction Ruta de larga distancia - en construcción
Hauptstraße Principal highway		Route principale Carretera principal
Nebenstraße Secondary road		Route secondaire Carretera secundaria
Fahrweg, Piste Practicable road, track		Chemin carrossable, piste Camino vecinal, pista
Straßennummerierung Road numbering	① 48 ① 26 26	Numérotage des routes Numeración de carreteras
Entfernungen in mi. (USA), in km (MEX) Distances in mi. (USA), in km (MEX)	259 130 129	Distances en mi. (USA), en km (MEX) Distancias en mi. (USA), en km (MEX)
Höhe in Meter - Pass Height in meters - Pass	1365	Altitude en mètres - Col Altura en metros - Puerto de montaña
Eisenbahn Railway		Chemin-de-fer Ferrocarril
Autofähre - Schifffahrtslinie Car ferry - Shipping route		Bac autos - Ligne maritime Transportador de automóviles - Ferrocarriles
Wichtiger internationaler Flughafen - Flughafen Major international airport - Airport	✈ ✈	Aéroport important international - Aéroport Aeropuerto importante internacional - Aeropuerto
Internationale Grenze - Bundesstaatengrenze International boundary - federal boundary		Frontière nationale - Frontière fédérale Frontera nacional - Frontera federal
Unbestimmte Grenze Undefined boundary		Frontière d'État non définie Frontera indeterminada
Zeitzonengrenze Time zone boundary	-4h Greenwich Time -3h Greenwich Time	Limite de fuseau horaire Límite del huso horario
Hauptstadt eines souveränen Staates National capital	**WASHINGTON**	Capitale nationale Capital de un estado soberano
Hauptstadt eines Bundesstaates State capital	**PHOENIX**	Capitale d'un état fédéral Capital de estado
Sperrgebiet Restricted area		Zone interdite Zona prohibida
Indianerreservat - Nationalpark Indian reservation - National park		Réserve d'indiens - Parc national Reserva de indios - Parque nacional
Sehenswertes Kulturdenkmal Interesting cultural monument	★ Disneyland	Monument culturel intéressant Monumento cultural de interés
Sehenswertes Naturdenkmal Interesting natural monument	⋆ Niagara Falls	Monument naturel intéressant Monumento natural de interés
Brunnen, Salzsee Well, Salt lake		Puits, Lac salé Pozo, Lago salado
MARCO POLO Erlebnistour 1 MARCO POLO Discovery Tour 1		MARCO POLO Tour d'aventure 1 MARCO POLO Recorrido aventura 1
MARCO POLO Erlebnistouren MARCO POLO Discovery Tours		MARCO POLO Tours d'aventure MARCO POLO Recorridos de aventura
MARCO POLO Highlight	★1	MARCO POLO Highlight

MARCO POLO TRAVEL GUIDES

Algarve
Amsterdam
Andalucia
Athens
Australia
Austria
Bali & Lombok
Bangkok
Barcelona
Berlin
Brazil
Bruges
Brussels
Budapest
Bulgaria
California
Cambodia
Canada East
Canada West / Rockies
& Vancouver
Cape Town &
Garden Route
Cape Verde
Channel Islands
Chicago & The Lakes
China
Cologne
Copenhagen
Corfu
Costa Blanca
& Valencia
Costa Brava
Costa del Sol & Granada
Crete
Cuba
Cyprus (North and
South)
Devon & Cornwall
Dresden
Dubai

Dublin
Dubrovnik &
Dalmatian Coast
Edinburgh
Egypt
Egypt Red Sea Resorts
Finland
Florence
Florida
French Atlantic Coast
French Riviera
(Nice, Cannes & Monaco)
Fuerteventura
Gran Canaria
Greece
Hamburg
Hong Kong & Macau
Iceland
India
India South
Ireland
Israel
Istanbul
Italy
Japan
Jordan
Kos
Krakow
Lake Garda
Lanzarote
Las Vegas
Lisbon
London
Los Angeles
Madeira & Porto Santo
Madrid
Mallorca
Malta & Gozo
Mauritius
Menorca

Milan
Montenegro
Morocco
Munich
Naples & Amalfi Coast
New York
New Zealand
Norway
Oslo
Oxford
Paris
Peru & Bolivia
Phuket
Portugal
Prague
Rhodes
Rome
Salzburg
San Francisco
Santorini
Sardinia
Scotland
Seychelles
Shanghai
Sicily
Singapore
South Africa
Sri Lanka
Stockholm
Switzerland
Tenerife
Thailand
Turkey
Turkey South Coast
Tuscany
United Arab Emirates
USA Southwest
(Las Vegas, Colorado,
New Mexico, Arizona
& Utah)
Venice
Vienna
Vietnam
Zakynthos & Ithaca,
Kefalonia, Lefkas

The travel guides with
Insider
Tips

INDEX

This index lists all sights, places and destinations plus several key terms and people featured in this guide. Numbers in bold indicate a main entry

Acuario Cayo Naranjo 111
Aldea Taína 80, **111**
Alto de Naranjo 92
Ancón 72
Baconao 87
Bahía de Bariay 80
Bahía de Cochinas (Bay of Pigs) **61**, 94
Bahía de Corrientes 53
Bahía Naranjo 80
Banes **78**, 103
Baracoa 16, 74, **75**, 102
Batista, Fulgencio 14, 15, 59, 69, 83, 103
Bayamo 17, **86**, 91, 92
Bioparque Rocazul 80
Birán **79**, 93, 100
Caleta Buena 61
Camagüey 62, **63**, 67, 91, 99, 113, 116
Capdevila 107
Cárdenas 60
Carpentier, Alejo 22, 44
Castro, Fidel 14, 15, 37, 40, 44, 45, 49, 56, 69, 74, 78, 79, 81, 82, 87, 93, 101, 102, 106, 114
Castro, Raúl 13, 14, 16, 40, 79, 100
Cayería del Norte 15, 62
Cayo Coco 62, 68, 69, 97, 98, 99, 111, 116
Cayo Ensenacho 62
Cayo Granma 81
Cayo Guillermo 62, 68, 69, 90, 91, 99, 104, 107, 110
Cayo Iguana 60
Cayo Jutías 55
Cayo Largo **60**, 106
Cayo Las Brujas 62, **71**, 91
Cayo Levisa **55**, 97
Cayo Media Luna 69, 100
Cayo Naranjo **79**, 111
Cayo Pájaro 60
Cayo Paredón Grande 68
Cayo Rico 60
Cayo Romano 68
Cayo Saetía **79**, 103
Cayo Santa María 62, 70, **71**
Céspedes, Manuel 86
Chivirico 87
Chorro de Maíta 80
Ciego de Ávila 62, **69**
Ciénaga de Zapata 16, 50, **60**, 94
Cienfuegos 63, **66**, 93, 106
Cienfuegos, Camilo 14, 37, 91
Cigars 31, 41

Cojímar **48**, 90
Columbus, Christopher 13, 14, 74, 75, 76, 80
Comandancia de la Plata (La) **86**, 92
Costa Esmeralda 78, 101
Costa Verde 78
Cueva de los Portales 53
Cueva de Punta del Este 49
Cueva del Indio **54**, 110
Cueva Finlay 49
Cueva Saturno 58
Cuevas de Bellamar 110
Diving 49, 58, 105
El Cobre **86**, 92, 113
Escambray Mountains 62, 66, **73**
Finca Mañacas 79, 100
Florida 99
Gibara **80**, 113
Girón 61
Gran Caverna de Santo Tomás 55
Gran Parque Natural Topes de Collantes **73**, 107
Guamá 60, 110
Guanahacabibes 50, 53
Guantánamo **77**, 102, 115
Guardalavaca **80**, 106, 107
Guevara, Ernesto „Che" 14, 24, 30, 35, 37, 40, 53, 62, 70, 91
Guillén, Nicolás 16, 64
Havanna 14, 17, 18, 19, 26, 30, **32**, 89, 94, 97, 107, 108, 109, 112, 113, 115, 116, 118, 120, 121
Hemingway, Ernest 17, 24, 26, 36, 37, 48, 107, 113
Holguín 15, 17, **78**, 93, 100, 103, 115, 116
Humboldt, Alexander von 16, 21, 39, 77
Humboldt National Park 16, **77**, 102, 107
Isla de la Juventud **49**, 60, 106
Jardín Botánico Cienfuegos 68
Jardines de la Reina 106
Jardines del Rey 15, 62, **68**, 91, 99, 100, 106
La Boca 60, 66, 94, 110
La Comandancia de La Plata **86**, 92
La Plata 86
Laguna Baconao 87
Laguna del Tesoro 60, 94

Las Terrazas **53**, 95, 104, 107
Los Guanos 80
Marea del Portillo **87**, 106
María La Gorda **52**, 106
Martí, José 39, 49, 77, 82
Matanzas 17, **61**, 90, 110
Mogotes 50, 54, 95
Moncada 55
Morón 68, **70**, 91, 98, 111
Mural de la Prehistoria 54
Music 31
Nueva Gerona 49
Palma Rubia 97
Parque de Baconao 87
Parque Monumento Nacional Bahía de Bariay 80
Parque Nacional Alejandro de Humboldt 16, **77**, 102, 107
Parque Nacional Desembarco del Granma 87
Parque Natural el Bagá 68
Pesquero 106
Pilón 87
Pinar del Río 50, **51**, 95
Playa Ancón 67
Playa Bacuranao 48
Playa Bibijagua 49
Playa Coral 58
Playa de los Cocos 66
Playa Esmeralda **80**, 107
Playa Girón **61**, 94
Playa Jibacoa 48
Playa Las Coloradas 87
Playa Pesquero 80
Playa Pilar 69, 100
Playa Rancho Luna 68
Playa Santa Lucía 62, **66**, 97, 98, 100, 106, 107
Playa Santa María 48
Playa Turquesa 80
Playa Yuragunal 80
Playas del Este 34, **48**, 90
Puente Bacunayagua 48, 89
Punta Francés 49
Remedios 17, **71**, 91, 113
Reserva Ecológica Varahicacos 57
Rum 26, 27, 31
San Diego de los Baños 50, **53**, 95
San Francisco de Paula 48
San Juan y Martínez 53
San Luis 53
Sancti Spíritus 17, **73**
Santa Clara 62, **70**, 91
Santa Isabel de las Lajas 113
Santiago de Cuba 17, 74, 75,

81, 87, 93, 101, 106, 111, 112, 113, 118
Santo Domingo 86, 91
Sierra de los Órganos 16, 50
Sierra del Rosario 50, 53
Sierra Maestra 74, 86
Sitio La Güira 111
Soroa **53**, 95
Tobacco 51, 52, 53

Topes de Collantes **73**, 107
Trinidad 17, 62, **72**, 93, 113
Valle de la Prehistoria 87, **111**
Valle de los Ingenios **72**, 93
Valle de Viñales 50, **54**, 95, 110
Valle Yumurí 48
Varadero 15, 34, 50, **56**, 90, 105, 107, 113, 116, 117

Vedado **43,** 117
Velázquez, Diego de 64, 72, 75, 81, 82
Vía Blanca 48
Viñales 16, **54**, 95, 104, 110, 116
Yaguajay 91

WRITE TO US

e-mail: info@marcopologuides.co.uk

Did you have a great holiday?
Is there something on your mind?
Whatever it is, let us know!
Whether you want to praise, alert us
to errors or give us a personal tip –
MARCO POLO would be pleased to
hear from you.
We do everything we can to provide
the very latest information for your trip.

Nevertheless, despite all of our authors'
thorough research, errors can creep
in. MARCO POLO does not accept any
liability for this. Please contact us by
e-mail or post.

MARCO POLO Travel Publishing Ltd
Pinewood, Chineham Business Park
Crockford Lane, Chineham
Basingstoke, Hampshire RG24 8AL
United Kingdom

PICTURE CREDITS
Cover Photograph:Varadero, beach (huber-images: H. - P. Huber)
Images: AWL Images: J. Arnold (10, 41, 49), W. Bibikow (44), A. Copson (4 top, 8), D. Delimont (flap right, 61), J. Sweeney (4 bottom, 23, 42, 59, 64, 70, 126/127); AWL Images/John Warburton-Lee Photography Ltd: N. Pavitt (6, 50/51, 52); DuMont Bildarchiv: Knobloch (54); R. M. Gill (31, 111, 114 bottom, 115); T. Hauser (112, 113); huber-images: Cossa (flap left), H. - P. Huber (1), S. Kremer (19 top, 32/33, 34, 38, 88/89), T. B. Morandi (12/13), Ripani (110), Schmid (9, 11, 14/15, 30/31, 62/63, 85), R. Schmid (2, 25, 81, 82, 86, 92); huber-images/SIME: M. Ripani (76), V. Sciosia (20/21); Look: Leue (36); mauritius images: U. Flüeler (18 centre, 29), F. Martin (99), L. Vallecillos (5); mauritius images/age (17); mauritius images/age fotostock: A. Cavalli (56/57); mauritius images/Alamy (7, 74/75, 79, 103, 114 top), K. Foy (96), M. Jucha (66); mauritius images/Alamy/photocay (106); mauritius images/Alamy/PJF Military Collection (18 top); mauritius images/Danita Delimont: B. Bachmann (73); mauritius images/FreshFood (28 right); mauritius images/Gastrofotos: C. Martinez Kempin (26/27); mauritius images/Imagebroker: N. Probst (104/105), P. Seyfferth (3); mauritius images/Maskot (18 bottom); Angel Ramírez (19 bottom); D. Renckhoff (69); T. Stankiewicz (28 left, 108/109); M. Thomas (30, 46, 112/113)

3ʳᵈ Edition – fully revised and updated 2019
Worldwide Distribution: Marco Polo Travel Publishing Ltd, Pinewood, Chineham Business Park, Crockford Lane, Basingstoke, Hampshire RG24 8AL, United Kingdom. Email: sales@marcopolouk.com
© MAIRDUMONT GmbH & Co. KG, Ostfildern
Chief editor: Marion Zorn; Author: Gesine Froese; Editor: Jochen Schürmann; Programme supervision: Lucas Forst-Gill, Susanne Heimburger, Johanna Jiranek, Nikolai Michaelis, Kristin Wittemann, Tim Wohlbold
Picture editor: Gabriele Forst; What's hot: Gesine Froese and wunder media, Munich; Cartography road atlas: © MAIRDUMONT, Ostfildern; Cartography pull-out map: © MAIRDUMONT, Ostfildern
Design front cover, p. 1, pull-out map cover: Karl Anders – Büro für Visual Stories, Hamburg; interior: milchhof:atelier, Berlin; Discovery Tours, p. 2/3: Susan Chaaban Dipl.-Des. (FH))
Translated from German by Susan Jones, Tübingen
Prepress: writehouse, Cologne; InterMedia, Ratingen
Phrase book in cooperation with Ernst Klett Sprachen GmbH, Stuttgart, Editorial by Pons Wörterbücher

MIX
Paper from
responsible sources
FSC® C124385

DOS & DON'TS ✋

A few handy hints to avoid common pitfalls on Cuba

DON'T FLAUNT YOUR MONEY

So far, Cuba still counted as a comparably safe country in Latin America. With the tourist boom, crime rates have unfortunately risen; thefts are more common than before. So: don't ever travel with all your cash on you, and don't flaunt what you do take, but distribute it over several parts of your body. The rest should remain in the hotel safe, as well as your passport – do however always have a copy with you.

DON'T EXPECT PERFECTION

Try to be patient! It's not only the slow socialist pace (with state employees) that can get on your nerves, it's also an infrastructure that, because of the tourist boom, is completely unable to cope: broken water pipes, overloaded electricity cables and prehistoric machines – and the perennial lack of this or that, e.g.paper for invoices or info materials. And who's to blame? Always the U.S. trade embargo!

DON'T SUNBATHE TOPLESS

In the eyes of many Cubans, going topless is a sign of European and North American moral decline. Those who cherish a seamless tan should keep this in mind. At the beaches of the all-inclusive resorts, topless bathing is tolerated. However, that's not where you'll find the Cubans (only as staff, though!).

DON'T SIT UNDER A COCONUT PALM

This is not a joke: Ten times more people die every year from falling coconuts than through shark attacks! Because when, at a height of 30 m/98 ft, a coconut starts to fall down, it can reach 50 mph and smash a human head or break your neck – because it is a damned hard nut.

DON'T GIVE CHILDREN MONEY

Children are not allowed to beg on Cuba: for one thing, none goes hungry (according to the state's assessment of things), and also successful begging undermines the work ethic. Still, many children like to hold out their hands when they see tourists. Most of all, avoid giving money. A lesser evil are small useful things such as ball-point pens.

DON'T THROW TOILET PAPER INTO THE TOILET

If you've travelled to other Third-World countries before, you'll already know this: used toilet paper must be thrown into the bin provided, not into the toilet bowl! The waste pipes have a smaller diameter than at home, and their downward slope is too flat. As a consequence, the toilets are easily blocked. Do your bit so that this doesn't happen!